"Neither the sure prevention of war nor the continuous use of world organisation will be gained without . . . the fraternal association of the English-speaking peoples. This means a special relationship. . . ."
—SIR WINSTON CHURCHILL *at Fulton, Missouri, March 3, 1946*

"The great causes and principles for which Britain and the United States have suffered and triumphed are not mere matters of the balance of power. They in fact involve the salvation of the world."
—SIR WINSTON CHURCHILL, *The Second World War,* Vol. VI

THE ALLIANCE OF NECESSITY

THE ALLIANCE

𝔰𝔡 STEIN AND DAY/*Publishers*/New York

OF NECESSITY

BRITAIN'S CRISIS, THE NEW EUROPE
AND AMERICAN INTERESTS

BY LIONEL GELBER

A NOTE OF ACKNOWLEDGMENTS

This work is a fresh statement of the writer's point of view. But here and there he has drawn upon ideas and material contributed by him to various periodicals on both sides of the Atlantic. He wishes to express his thanks to those publications for allowing that to be done. The British periodicals that have been good enough to grant such permission are the *Statist, Contemporary Review, European Review,* and the *Monthly Bulletin* of the Commonwealth Industries Association. American publications to which the writer is similarly indebted are *Foreign Affairs* (an article copyrighted by the Council on Foreign Relations, Inc., New York), *Worldview* (Council on Religion and International Affairs) and *Orbis* (Foreign Policy Research Institute, University of Pennsylvania).

Stein and Day/*Publishers*/7 East 48 Street, New York, N. Y. 10017

PREFACE

This book has been written to express the belief that, while Britain can find a middle stance between primacy and decline, her role would be diminished, not enlarged, by entry into "Europe."

As center of the Commonwealth and as chief ally of the United States, Britain, despite grave domestic ills, still has an important part to play in the free world. Europeanization, by its very nature, would not permit her to play that part.

The case must first be stated in the light of world trends and the impact of the new Europe on American leadership. The very fact that many Britons seek Europeanization calls for a survey of what has altered in the British outlook and British society—and of what remains unaltered. For an improvement in Britain's prospects, two things are needed: internal reforms and recognition by the United States that, if she is to rely on Britain as a close ally, she must help the British find an alternative to Europeanization.

It can be done. Yet there will be no urge to do it unless fundamentals are reconsidered on both sides of the Atlantic. And it is with a plea for such a reconsideration that the argument of the book is rounded out.

This plea is based on a view of world trends set forth

in the early pages of this work and returned to in the latter sections. A few preliminary remarks may be made here:

Tension between major nuclear Powers has relaxed when the two rival camps of East and West each are split within. For Russia, perhaps even for Communist China, war has ceased to be a rational instrument of policy. But American power, with the support of NATO, is what has been the great persuader—what has insured a reprieve from war. The United States and Britain on the one hand and the Soviet Union on the other have yet to take the sharp edge off East-West competition. They will have intractable allies to deal with as they proceed.

Not that they will be proceeding at once. Strife in Vietnam has been one overt cause of delay; attempts by Moscow and Peking to subvert new African regimes has been another. The stake in the concurrent Soviet quarrel with the Communist Chinese has been Russia's place in the world. The Kremlin's problem has never been a simple one—to maintain the arms race and the race in space when Soviet agriculture is still so backward and so many consumer needs have still to be met. Russia might, nevertheless, have taken such adversities in her stride if the countervailing defenses of the West had not also restrained her; if the West had not set bounds beyond which she dared not go. But other burdens must have seemed all the more daunting when, after Allied rights were upheld in Berlin, Soviet missiles had to be removed from Cuba; when the Kennedy-Khrushchev showdown indicated that Russia could not break out of the global box in which she had been wedged. Only through an accommodation with the West can she get lasting relief. The power contest could thus put a curb upon itself, and if it does, the West, by exercising its power for peace, will again have vindicated its use of power.

A limited détente would in itself enable mankind to draw an easier breath. But while Russia and the West might settle some of their differences, that would not be the same as a durable peace. And no durable peace can be achieved until Russia abandons political warfare against the West, until she modifies a concept of peaceful coexistence under which the West may still be communized—even though (as with the minor wars subsidized in Africa and Asia) it would be by methods short of all-out nuclear war. A limited détente might provide Russia with a free rein for waging political warfare; and yet it could also be a cushioned trap. For once the Kremlin softened the rigors of the cold war, it would be difficult, at home and abroad, to reimpose them.

As for the West, it has a relative advantage which, if it thinks things out afresh, even a loss in solidarity will not erase. It must, however, think things out afresh. In the reconstruction of Europe, the good still seems to outweigh the bad. But the new Europe would have posed a challenge to the English-speaking peoples even if they had not had General de Gaulle to conjure with, or even if he had been more demure. His successors may do less to trouble them and their allies in the sphere of defense. Yet the English-speaking peoples will be more troubled by politico-economic problems which, as European integration is resumed, the new Europe is bound to raise.

It is one purpose of this work to serve as a reminder of that neglected truth. The writer devoted a previous book to the theme of American leadership and the British role.[1] It was written in New York where he was living when the postwar programs of the United States were hammered out. This new, shorter book is devoted to the European phase of British policy and to the British

1. *America in Britain's Place*, Frederick A. Praeger, Inc. (New York, 1961; Allen and Unwin, London, 1961).

phase of American policy in Europe. It was written in London where the writer lived during and after the campaign for British entry into the Common Market.

Much on the British scene was familiar. The writer, a Canadian, went up to Oxford two years before Hitler attained office and lived in London until the eve of the Munich Agreement. It was in London that the writer, taking world politics as a contest for power, pointed (in an article published before the fall of Austria) to the danger of a Nazi-Soviet Pact and insisted (in a prewar book) upon Anglo-American friendship as the main hope of civilized society. That was not the way to win favor on the Left, Right, or Center. But it was with the experience of those prewar years in mind that the writer has watched at close range another great debate on Britain's future.

There has been no exact precedent for the West's inner disorder or for the disarray in which the East finds itself. But that is all the more reason for clinging to elements of whose worth the past gave proof. Vital elements would, nevertheless, have been relinquished if Britain had entered the Common Market; and will be if, in years to come, she does.

Since the 1930's the British world role has altered, and so has the American stake in it. But it should not be altered more than necessary; there should be no gratuitous impairment. Yet that is what the result would be— such is the argument of this volume—if Britain joined "Europe."

Exponents of British membership in the Common Market feel their ideas have been borne out by yet another trade and monetary crisis in Britain. It is the contention of this work, however, that their entire approach is a mistaken one. In Paris, as in London, governments change; what does not change is the desire of many, on both sides of the Channel and on both sides of the Atlantic, to have Britain occupy a chair at the conference table of the Common Market in Brussels. Yet that unvarying objective might not be in the British or American interest, or in the interest of the West. This book will try to suggest why that is so and what the United States as well as Britain may have to do about the new Europe.

There has, of course, been no dearth of comment on the economic aspects of these questions. But what is signified from a broad political standpoint? That is something few statesmen and opinion media in Britain and the United States have been willing to explore.

An attempt to fill the gap should therefore be made. Most of what has been said in print and on the air has favored British entry into the Common Market. The case against such a step may, on that ground alone, now be entitled to a wider hearing.

Disarray in the West is the general background against which this whole topic must be studied. A cry has been raised for a re-examination of the premises on which the accepted policies of the West have rested. None require more of a reappraisal, agonizing or un-agonizing, than those that come up for discussion in these pages.

One final introductory word should be added. Events may, with the passage of time, furnish other data. The same arguments will apply. This book is not a news report. It has been written as an analysis of basic issues, and they persist.

LIONEL GELBER

CONTENTS

1

EUROPE AND AMERICA
The General Situation

I A MARRIAGE OF INCONVENIENCE

It is hard to imagine a free world in which Britain would
no longer have an individual capacity. It is also hard to
see how she can keep one if she becomes an integral part
of a European union. Until World War II Britain's individual capacity was something Americans took for
granted. But now they have assumed that they could deal
more easily with Western Europe if Britain merged her
political identity with it. An individual British capacity is,
nevertheless, still an element with which the United
States, as leader of the West, cannot dispense. For a step
designed to stabilize Western Europe could have a wider
destabilizing effect.

This is not the only point that those who study the
British role will have to ponder. But when the Europeanization of Britain is proposed, they must also ask what
"Europe" will be like. And that in turn brings up the
problem of its attitude toward the United States. The
new Europe cannot stand alone. Its relations with the
United States must therefore be scrutinized first of all.

Europe and America are like a married couple who
seem unable to live happily together and yet cannot live
apart. In the old days the marriage, so far as it derived

13

from mutual interest rather than a romantic attachment, might have been described as a marriage of convenience. But a marriage of inconvenience would be a more apt description of a match in which partners who, though incompatible in many respects, are welded so closely together. It is consoling that wedded bliss is not conspicuous in the Sino-Soviet household either. There is solace, too, in the fact that domestic friction dwindles when the West is challenged from without. But it is not only against a chronic threat from the East that the West has had to close ranks and take its own disarray in hand.

Two of the recent stages in the marriage of Europe and America are familiar enough—Europe spurned by America between the wars, America striving so bountifully after World War II to bring Europe back to life. Now another stage has been reached. West Europeans have been feeling less dependent on America than before and the idea of separation, if not divorce, has been in the air. The Common Market did a lot to further it even though that experiment has not been going ahead as many hoped it would. Trends toward the unification of Western Europe have, for the moment, been suspended. But when they again develop, the United States will have to reconsider some neglected fundamentals and so will Britain.

To check the disruptive and stress the cohesive—such is the task confronting the United States as leader of the West. The late President Kennedy, borrowing a theme from Messrs. Eisenhower and Macmillan, suggested a Declaration of Interdependence. In a celebrated speech on July 4, 1962, Kennedy announced that the United States would be ready to discuss ways and means of forming a concrete Atlantic partnership with a united Europe. He envisaged it as not only fortifying the defense of the free world, but as looking outward to cooperate with all nations in meeting common concerns. President Kennedy did not add that an inward-looking Europe might aggravate rather than allay current perplexities. But it well might.

II PEACE BY POWER

Defense may not be the sole realm in which the destiny of free nations is decided, but unless they prevail there, others will. The isolationists and appeasers of the past and the pacifists and neutralists of the present have been reluctant to admit this basic truth. It is, all the same, not by dodging the realities of power that free societies perpetuate themselves. In how good a position is Europe now to fend for itself? Will it be more able than it has been to set the terms for Atlantic interdependence? Peace-keeping in the postwar world has been mainly the duty of the United States. And there is no sign that "Europe" would do as much even if it could.

How is peace kept? The major wars of the twentieth century might have been prevented if, when threats first arose, the Atlantic peoples had seen that there was a free-world order to preserve; if they had realized in good time how they would have to combine if a free-world order were to be preserved without conflict. During World War I that free-world order could still best be preserved by maintaining the balance of power in Europe. Since Pearl Harbor, the area of wartime conflict has been enlarged and so, since World War II, has the scope of postwar competition. Peace has been maintained by a global balance of power, underwritten for the West by the United States.

Europe, while still a most crucial area in the global structure, is but one among several others. During the nineteenth century the *Pax Britannica* profited from Britain's world-wide command of the seas and a favorable balance of power in Europe. All this has passed away. In the second half of the twentieth century, Europeans have not been able to uphold by themselves the European segment of a global equilibrium. That is why a North American presence in NATO Europe has served as more than a symbol and supplement. What makes this presence so formidable is the fact that it is part of a global power structure of which the nuclear sea and air power of the United States is the world-wide prop.

That is not the whole story. Although nobody in the nuclear-missile age can win a major war, the free world without such arms would lose its freedom. Peace by power is thus still the watchword of the West. But as East and West deter each other in the military sphere, they compete all the harder in the nonmilitary sphere. Furthermore, the distribution of power between the rival camps has not merely brought forth an East-West equilibrium. Interior forces within each camp get from this equilibrium a certain latitude for asserting themselves. Critics of American leadership, allied and neutralist, have been rendered secure by that which they criticize. Those who are fair-minded should not be bracketed with the uninformed or ill-disposed. But the process that has arrested adversaries of the West has, as it were, also unmuzzled some of its beneficiaries.

There would have been no need to court neutralists as they have been courted if so large a portion of the struggle between antagonistic concepts of world order, the free and the Communist one, had not shifted to the nonmilitary sphere. As it was, some of the relatively powerless states acquired a chance to speak as though they possessed substantial power. The more colossi vie for power, the greater the strength of the weak. But within the West itself there has been no basic redistribution of power. Not even a Gaullist Europe could safely extort one as long as it must rely on global power guarantees to which the United States still contributes most.

(These power guarantees, moreover, are what have enabled the United Nations to persevere although the world body has been hobbled by the East-West contest, by the strength of the weak, which is one outcome of that contest, and by the West's own disarray. No permanent international police force has even been feasible, and it is only within the strategic ambit of the West that the United Nations could make itself useful. The United States, with a handful of allies, fought the Korean War under the flag of the world body. In policing trouble spots the record of the United Nations has been uneven. And dissension over *ad hoc* ventures, after wracking the world body politically, has also emptied its coffers. This is not to belittle what, within limits, the United Nations has accomplished. To the mechanics of peace-keeping, it is a necessary adjunct. But as it cannot itself keep the peace in any global sense, its own use of the term "peace-keeping" may be overdone.)

Nor does the world equilibrium induce the same kind of change across the board. Soviet client States must still be more circumspect than those who, though unaligned, have the power of the West as their shield of national independence. And the Gaullist French have not been as rambunctious in the West as the Communist Chinese have been in the East. Russia and China have been reshuffling their cards, and the manner in which they adapt themselves to each other must also impinge profoundly on the prospects of the West.

III STATUS VERSUS DEFENSE

A dispute over the command of the nuclear deterrent has reflected disparities of power within the Western Alliance. It has also reflected changes in the very nature of military power.

Can Europe be embroiled without America or can America be embroiled without Europe? Definitely not. Such immunity is ruled out by war plans, by modern war technology, by the world-wide range of the East-West contest itself, by a strategic interlock—by the fact that, as any adversary must regard the defense system of the West as a single mechanism, he will mount his assaults accordingly.

The reconstruction of its economy, therefore, will not remove Western Europe from the line of fire (to do that it would have to contract out of its alliance with America and knuckle under to Moscow). The allies were worried during the Korean War and by subsequent events in the Far East about the degree to which they were meshed with the United States in a strategic interlock. Today that might worry the United States herself.

There were, from the standpoint of Britain and the West, two dangers during the Korean War and its aftermath. The first was that Western Europe would be abandoned to Soviet conquest or coercion if the United States, rash and stiff-necked, was bogged down in the Far East. Secondly, there was fear that the British Isles at the opposite corner of the earth might be engulfed in-

directly because of some air-atomic action taken by the
United States in East Asian skies. For Russia could have
honored her security pact with Communist China by
striking back in Europe at Britain, the chief ally of the
United States. But President Truman, as architect of the
Western coalition, saw that the Korean struggle had to
be localized. The Communist Chinese may have signed
an armistice only when President Eisenhower intimated
that he might use nuclear weapons, and he might have
used them in 1958 when Peking seemed about to pounce
on the Nationalist offshore islands of Quemoy and Matsu.
In the end, President Eisenhower like all of President
Truman's successors followed the line that he set.

Now the boot is on the other foot. It is not American
trigger-happiness that frightens many in Western Europe
but a hypothetical American timidity—the fear that, to
avert a nuclear counterattack on North America, the
United States, in some European emergency, will back
away.

On other fronts, however, an American forward policy
is still the last thing that Europeans desire. Their appre-
hensions would have been revived if Senator Goldwater
had defeated President Johnson. And the Vietnamese
imbroglio has rekindled some of the anxieties of the
1950's. Not even the United States can back away and,
at the same time, involve allies without their consent.
The fallacy that she may do both is, all the same, part
of the Gaullist self-justification for the French sabotage
of NATO. But the tables will have turned if, on the continent of Europe as much as in the Orient, a watch
against trigger-happiness has to be kept.

Is it likely that in a European emergency the United
States would do too little rather than too much? Britain
did not wish to be caught short and that was one of her

motives when she built her own deterrent. France has
also built her own deterrent. It is improbable, however,
that the French deterrent will be co-ordinated as closely
as the British deterrent has been with the over-all American deterrent. Nor will the United States be as willing
to entrust nuclear secrets to France. The French themselves cannot tell what kind of regime they will have to
which information, so vital for the defense of the West,
might have to be imparted. But with their flair for invok-
ing reason to mask unreason, the French demand that
the United States and Britain have more faith in them
than they, before, during and since Vichy, have had in
each other.

In a unified Europe, the French might or might not
share the direction of their nuclear deterrent with others.
The French deterrent could be a vehicle not only for
achieving equality for Western Europe but for ensuring
France's pre-eminence in Western Europe. The budgetary
costs, however, would be astronomical for any French
Government. And if Europeans beggar themselves to
attain a full complement of nuclear arms, it might well
be that they could not attain parity in other respects.

Europe and America are bound to argue over these
differing estimates of future contingencies as long as the
East-West contest lasts. A unified Europe, regional in
ambit, would desire equal access to the levers of a global
power apparatus that only the United States, among the
nations of the West, has had the means to create and
keep up. There may be no room on the trigger for more
than one finger. But what if there is more than one
trigger?

There might, in fact, be more than one trigger if
there is a European deterrent which is not co-ordinated
with the over-all American deterrent. An alternative

would be to assign the European deterrent to NATO
where it could, perhaps, be run by Europeans and Americans together. As long as a NATO deterrent is co-ordinated with the over-all American deterrent, the United
States may still exercise ultimate control over the nuclear
defense of the West. But if it were not so co-ordinated,
how safe would the West be?

There will have to be wider participation in advance
planning. Contingency planning during the Berlin crisis
of 1961 may have shown the way. And there can be more
of this without a mixed-manned NATO Nuclear Force
being established. The White House may assign nuclear
authority to a NATO commander as circumstances require. France has rejected an American proposal for a
special committee of defense ministers. Russia has been
against anything that may give the Bonn Republic a
voice in the control of nuclear weaponry. Other methods
to improve consultation within the Western Alliance
might, however, be found.

In principle it is right that European allies should
want full equality of status with the United States. But
what still rules this out is the character of the new war
technology, the risks it entails for the entire human race.
Equality of status will not be worth much if a strategic
interlock is mismanaged. It may be mismanaged if its
ultimate control passes into other hands.

Nor should there be uncertainty about American attitudes. The signs could also be read for other regions
when the late President Kennedy took his stand against
Soviet missiles in Cuba and when President Johnson took
measured reprisals against North Vietnam. The influences
to which a unified Europe, as a nuclear equal, might be
subjected are more uncertain. The all-encompassing
range of the East-West contest itself would, at any rate,

remain a potent compulsion for the United States to act. Western Europe has from the outset been the chief prize of that world contest. If the Communist East were to acquire sway over Western Europe—with its human resources, its physical plant, its central strategic position— the global balance of power would shift irretrievably against the United States.

Europeans might recall that during the two world wars Europe was nearly lost before the United States came to the rescue. American leadership and the new global balance of power are not alone in having altered all that. The very nature of nuclear weapons has also altered it. Europe could not be regained without being simultaneously expunged from the map. To be held, Europe must be held here and now.

The United States, in other words, could not retire from Western Europe and suppose that she could again return to liberate it if necessary. When the ravages of modern war cannot be undone, they must be forestalled, and to forestall them the Western Alliance must be prepared to meet such contingencies, nuclear and non-nuclear, regional as well as global, as may arise. Between the overall American deterrent and the American presence in Europe the link has been clear.

There may, moreover, have been reassurance by events. The Kennedy-Khrushchev showdown over Cuba, when the two global colossi had their first direct confrontation, was a postwar turning point from two salient angles. It revealed the size of the European stake in the hemispheric security of the United States. But it did something else as well. When the United States upheld the world balance in her own immediate sector, she also rendered the European sector more secure.

What this meant may be restated in other terms.

When the American people backed a firm Kennedy stance in their own theater, they served notice on Moscow and Peking that the intimidation of so important a theater as Western Europe would also be withstood. What more can Europe ask? Can it be sure, when its own record is examined, that it would do as much for itself?

Twice, in a phrase more prescient than Canning himself could appreciate, the New World has been called into existence to redress the balance of the Old. But now the New World has called the Old World into existence to redress a balance that extends to the limits of the earth. No reversal of roles could be functionally more significant, and it is in this light that Europeans must assess it.

The time has come, moreover, for Americans themselves to reassess it. Headshaking over setbacks in Southeast Asia and sub-Sahara Africa is natural enough. Yet American leadership, on the whole, has been no failure. How to make a success of success: that, when even lesser human undertakings fall short, is the American dilemma.

The United States could not, at any rate, intervene on all sectors or intervene everywhere in depth—nor could her choice of elements always be the same. It is in the air and not on land that America is supreme. From the standpoint of the West, the security of some regions is more vital than that of others. Undue retrenchment would not permit the United States to uphold a global balance at all—World War II made that apparent. The Korean War demonstrated that America must not overextend herself if she is to bring power to bear where it matters most.

And the defense of Western Europe is what has determined American priorities beyond the Western Hemisphere. A number of West Europeans have, nevertheless, been loath to acknowledge what the new global balance entailed—its greater dimensions, the degree to which these have had to be ascertained experimentally, by trial and error. Some in Western Europe, feeling relegated to the side lines of the world contest, still fancy themselves more detached from the global balance than the facts warrant. With the growth of the Common Market, many Europeans became engrossed in another kind of expansion—that of a semicontinental economy. Intercontinental, nonetheless, is the scale of the underpinnings by which the new Europe has been kept secure.

And that is why Western Europeans as well as Americans should employ global yardsticks. It is true they may not bring perfect amity in the West much nearer by doing this. Generally, however, those who employ the same global yardsticks may be less prone than they have been to talk past each other, to pursue what the French call a *dialogue des sourds*. Western Europeans mirror the spirit of the times when they seek a closer integration among themselves. But they may lag behind the times when their stake in the global balance is minimized.

How, it will be asked, is the European sector of that global balance still to be held? There may be less and less need for American air bases overseas as intercontinental missiles pile up and as Polaris submarines, invulnerable with their second-strike capacity, are deployed around the Sino-Soviet imperium. The American presence in Europe is a special case. In addition to being part of the over-all deterrent, it has a specific local purpose. Allies may bicker with the United States over how the European ramparts of the West may best be manned, but an American withdrawal from Europe is not in the cards.

For here, again, it is the stark, unrelenting exigencies of a global balance that must shape American policy. A voluntary American pull-out from Western Europe would not be in the American national interest.

Doubts about the American response to any final crisis still linger, nevertheless, among the transatlantic allies of the United States. These have lent impetus to French and even West German aspirations in the nuclear field. Yet the over-all American deterrent is always there to bank upon, and it is because the Sino-Soviet bloc has been deterred by this that West Europeans have felt scant need to augment their *conventional* forces. American pleas to have them augmented are deemed a further sign that the United States, rather than expose American cities to nuclear retaliation, would never employ major nuclear weapons even as a last resort.

The East-West stalemate generated by these weapons has certainly not been to the detriment of Western Europe. And a similar stalemate in the domain of conventional warfare is what, in the American view, NATO allies could do more to achieve. Without a further stalemate in the domain of conventional warfare, the entire machinery of nuclear deterrence might be undermined. West Germany is contributing more than the others toward achieving such a stalemate—but the ground on which Bonn does this is less strategic than political.

There cannot be more stress on NATO's conventional defenses when cooperation with NATO by France runs low. What the French have wanted instead is to remove the over-all American deterrent from exclusive American control. And this they have tried to do by forming a nuclear armory of their own.

The French nuclear deterrent, it is evident, may be

less independent technically than its builders admit.[1] Operationally, however, it may be more independent than others yet realize. For through it, France, and any associated with her, might acquire an oblique command over the American deterrent itself—a French or European deterrent being able, such is the strategic interlock, to spark the over-all American deterrent even against American wishes.

This point should be scrutinized from yet another angle. By itself a smaller European deterrent might or might not have capacity to stave off a nuclear mammoth like the Soviet Union. What would make a European deterrent a more formidable tool of policy is the extent to which it could involve still larger elements of power. Western Europe, in other words, may try to correct the nuclear disparity between itself and the United States; but when it does so, it may also vitiate any correlation between power and responsibility. For while the United States still pays the piper, Western Europe may eventually call the tune.

1. The Paris correspondent of *The Economist* (London, April 25, 1964) provided two illustrations of that point. The first was "the strange case of *Machines Bull*, an electronics firm allegedly so essential for national development that the (French) Government would not allow it to be touched by foreign hands. Now it has been forced to accept the assistance of the American General Electric Company. The second was the confirmation of earlier reports that not only is the *force de frappe* dependent on American flying tankers for refueling, but that the new Mirages carrying French atom bombs will be powered by American jet engines."

For the British deterrent, co-ordinated as it had been with the over-all American deterrent, no absolute independence in these spheres had ever been proclaimed.

Enriched uranium for the first French nuclear submarine was to be, but has not been, obtained from the United States. France is to have a squadron of submarines armed with Polaris missiles. Meanwhile, her nuclear bombers, though vulnerable, can be refueled in flight by 12 American jet tankers.

Gaullist France cannot do without American military supplies and spare parts. It is, above all, essential that the French deterrent have at its disposal NATO's integrated radar network.

Despite the din of controversy, there has been silence over another grim aspect of the nuclear problem. If war should come, the havoc wrought in an age of intercontinental weapons might be much the same on both sides of the Atlantic. How, then, can the rulers of Western Europe be any less subject to inhibitions that, according to West Europeans, might cause an American President to falter and vacillate? Paris and Bonn may no longer entrust their destiny in all respects to Washington, while Washington and Ottawa may be loath to have their destiny decided by Paris and Bonn. And in a strictly Western context there might be no solution to the problem. Its global ramifications are, however, what make the problem so acute. It would be less acute if, having been put in a global context, it could be circumvented.

That might be done through an understanding between Russia and the West. But the quest for such an understanding has also been stirring up fresh misunderstanding within the West itself. A détente between Russia and the West would solidify the status quo. For reasons of their own, France and West Germany have not wanted the status quo to be solidified, but their individual interests and the general interest may not be the same.

Even as Paris and Bonn might quarrel with Washington and London about this, discord between the French and the West Germans can also arise. France has presupposed that her own nuclear predominance in Western Europe will be more than a match for the conventional predominance of the Bonn Republic. But how sure can the French be that the Bonn Republic will long accept nuclear disparity within the West European fold?

Germany's unsettled future is, at any rate, what keeps much else unsettled. And there was alarm on both sides of the Iron Curtain when Washington proposed a multi-

lateral nuclear fleet in which Bonn's share might have
been disproportionate.

From all this two conclusions may be deduced. The
first is that no one can escape from the strategic interlock.
The second is that the United States will cease to be the
sole manager of that interlock if a European deterrent
can set the American deterrent in motion—something it
could do by the reprisals it might invite. But it is not only
in the West that nuclear controls will, for weal or woe,
be decentralized. Decentralization in the East could make
things as difficult for Russia as does decentralization in
the West for the United States.

Yet dissidents should have less capacity for mischief
with a détente between Russia and the West—it then
being more possible to localize any damage they can do.
Although smaller deterrents may touch off larger ones
through the roundabout strategic interlock with which
the war machines of East and West have been endowed,
an all-engulfing holocaust may be averted if nuclear giants
have reassured each other beforehand. And so, by their
nuclear undertakings, Paris and Peking may have rendered one unwitting service. The need for an accord
between nuclear giants (together with Britain) is made
all the more evident.

A tacit nuclear equilibrium maintains peace. To upset
this global equilibrium, as decentralized nuclear controls
would upset it, is to render peace still less secure. That
is why the more centralized the nuclear controls, the
safer (under the conditions of a strategic interlock) mankind will be. And that, too, is why an agreement against
the spread of nuclear weapons, similar to the partial
nuclear test ban, will not be enough. An agreement to
bypass the decentralizers—Gaullist France, Communist
China, lesser nuclear aspirants—may also be required.

Not that such an agreement will be so urgent if, beyond joint targeting, other forms of co-ordination can be arranged between the French *force de frappe* and the Strategic Air Command of the United States—if, even more, the Communist Chinese adopt a less defiant posture. In the meantime, what Russia and the West cannot tolerate is that nuclear dissidents might have them—and, with them, the whole of mankind—at their mercy. The imperatives of survival, such is modern war technology, cut across competing ideologies. And it is by these imperatives that nuclear giants should be impelled.

Politically, of course, there is no resemblance between dissidents. The French and Chinese do not subscribe to the same concepts of world order, but the global effect is the same when France, by adding to the spread of nuclear weapons, does strategically what Communist China has been doing. Yet the regional strategy of these two dissidents is very different. The French, trying to erect a pedestal for themselves, now hinder the defense of the West; in the East, the two chief allies treat each other as enemies. The degree to which post-Gaullist France will uphold Gaullist objectives in Europe and the West is conjectural, but whatever reveals defects in those objectives must tend to restore France to the comity of the West. The split between Communist behemoths is much deeper than the Western split as the Chinese extend their sway in East Asia and exhort the colored multitudes of the earth to follow them instead of their predominantly white Soviet rival. Upon Russia the countervailing pressure of the West has thus had assistance from an unexpected quarter.

As an air-atomic Power, Communist China may still lack a full complement of delivery systems, but there is political utility in the mere possession of nuclear weapons.

These can be used to overawe weaker neighbors, wear down India, and impress other Afro-Asian developing countries. It is as a land power, however, that Communist China is so formidable—having the ability, with so large a population, to recruit and equip huge land armies.

Against this Chinese land power, Russia may yet have to move more conventional forces from her European to her Asian frontiers. A limited détente with the West could expedite such a transference although the German status quo has not been accepted and, until it is, large garrisons of Russian troops will have to be kept in or near Eastern Europe. One thing is patent. There can be no comprehensive scheme of disarmament without a decrease in conventional arms and in East Asia, at any rate, an increase is more likely.

The Powers cannot disarm or disengage in one sphere without affecting other spheres, and here political attitudes will always be the key. The atmosphere between Russia and the West has tended to improve. This tendency, even when slowed down, must be maintained—though its conversion into specific arrangements for disarmament in the nuclear or conventional fields may be held up or will, at best, be haphazard. And tacit self-denying ordinances are what might help to maintain it.

Meanwhile, dissidence in the East has been having the heavier impact on the global balance. Communist China, by her revolt against the white industrialized "haves," has done all she could do to revolutionize the East-West contest itself. While Russia and the West might stand on guard against each other, they also will have to stand on guard, in varying degrees of proximity, against a common threat.

Never has there been a problem for statecraft that, wheels within wheels, is at once so vast, so far-reaching and so intricate. The West cannot put its power to good use as well as it should if Europe and America are set apart and if, as the reconstruction of Europe proceeds, the role of Britain is misconstrued.

IV AMERICA AND AMERICANIZATION

Europe may come to be more highly integrated than most Europeans yet realize. Resting upon a customs union and an economic union, the new European edifice is to be rounded out by a political union. And that is not surprising, since the modern politico-economy cannot be separated into watertight compartments. What happens where barriers still constrict? Quite pragmatically, and without resort to doctrine, the integrative powers of the state may come into play. If state powers are needed to get things done across the length and breadth of Western Europe, then a larger statehood may swallow up component states under one label or another.

And that is why European federalists can wait with comparative serenity for President de Gaulle to vanish from the scene. A union of states such as he proposed may not long withstand the pressure for closer integration that a unified Europe must generate of its own accord. Other partners, even at this early stage, could not withdraw from the Common Market when France, brushing them imperiously aside, blackballed Britain, for a point of no return had already been passed.

France later boycotted the Common Market when she did not get her own way. The Common Market has, nevertheless, remained a going concern. But it cannot do so without the process of integration being resumed. Nothing much came of the Franco-German Treaty of Co-operation when General de Gaulle got on less well with Dr. Erhard than he had with Herr Adenauer. And no progress toward political union was made within Europe after Britain had been barred. Yet the more stubborn the obstacles, the greater the likelihood that only supranational powers will suffice for surmounting them.

An American prototype has shown the shape of things to come. Trade is not the only sphere in which the example set by the United States may prefigure the future of Europe. The Common Market does what the United States did when she organized a customs union in a semi-continental expanse, when, removing tariffs among insiders, she made them uniform against outsiders. By the same token, a unified Europe may have to do what the United States did in all other branches of the American economy. Among free societies she is the most successful pioneer of bigness. And as with her, so with the Common Market—the greater the flow of European trade, the tighter the grip of bigness on the European economy. But it cannot tighten that grip without deepening the general pattern of European integration.

Trade and bigness interact. When they do, the ground is cleared for that federal merger through which alone the full potentialities of the entire venture can best be fulfilled. The paths taken may be diverse, uneven, circuitous, without the usual signposts. The European communities might provide novel modalities. It may be that within a political union there can be no outright pooling of sovereignty without the consent of members, but what members cannot do is delimit the energies that a customs union will have released and that an economic union will have quickened on an ever-enlarging scale. Although deep-seated particularisms in language and culture might still impede, they could be bypassed as a unified Europe consolidated itself indivisibly.

The United States has given her blessing to the closest integration of Europe, economic and political. But would she be pleased if, as the many are replaced by one, particularism is not banished? If, as applied to defense, diplomacy, world trade, and international finance, European particularism is merely projected on a larger screen? The irony of that for the United States would be evident.

It is expected that a unified Europe will have the ability to say "no" in unison to the United States as well as "yes." The desired unison may be achieved on an American model. In other words, the more American techniques are assimilated, the more capable Europeans will be of resisting American counsels. And so it might not only be postwar subsidies from the United States that will have helped a unified Europe to diverge from America. The processes by which America herself was Americanized, as it were, also will help.

This paradox should be understood. The United States could never have Americanized others by her own unaided efforts. But when others emulate America and the American style of life—based on mass production coupled with a free movement of trade, people, and classes in a semicontinental area—they may Americanize themselves. A unified Europe will give bigness a greater chance in a region that historically has prided itself on its rejection of bigness. A European Third Force might be one outcome.

This is not to argue against the new Europe or against the form it will take. But it is in the light of federalizing trends that the proposal for British participation should be reconsidered. An integrated Europe will constitute a sum greater than its parts. Only as the parts subordinate themselves to the whole can integration proceed. A change of the most basic character would thus have been set on foot—one that Britain could not undergo and still keep a role of her own. A role of her own is, however, not only in Britain's own interest but, as Washington might yet realize, in the American interest and in that of many others as well. It has generally been assumed that, by participating in the processes of European integration, Britain could alter them. Her own status, as a matter of fact, is what would be altered.

V A THIRD FORCE?

Political auguries for the new Europe are mixed. The French and Germans deserve the thanks of mankind for burying the hatchet, but the underlying goals of the two peoples still are not the same. Territorially, at any rate, France is a satisfied power, while the Bonn Republic, like Germany between the wars, is a dissatisfied one. From Bismarck to Hitler, the two postwar Germanies were a single state for less than seventy-five years. And for their partition between East and West the German people have only themselves to blame.

The West has had to champion claims for German reunification so as to keep the Bonn Republic well disposed toward the West.[1] On other grounds, however, Western statesmen should have hesitated to endorse this objective. The reunion of the two Germanies can be achieved only on terms that would disrupt the Common

1. "The unity of the German people," declared Herr Ludwig Erhard on June 17, 1963, "remains an eternal value." Will this "eternal" value (apart from East Germany with or without the Oder-Neisse lands) also include Austria and the Sudetenland as it did between the wars?

Market and undo the pending unification of Western Europe. The West, moreover, has the West European sector of a global equilibrium to defend. German reunification would be in conflict with that paramount task.

It is through a divided Germany that NATO lines have been drawn, and upon which, despite much said to the contrary, the West has predicated the security of Western Europe. But none of that would be feasible if the Bonn Republic became part of a neutral Reich—in which situation it could no longer add strength to the West or have allies upon whom territorial advantages might be bestowed. Would it not, therefore, pay Russia, with East Germany in thrall, to let her combine with West Germany—even if the latter shunned the Communist system?

A neutral Reich, in which the Soviet Union permitted a satellite to rejoin the Bonn Republic, could deny the West strategic access to German soil and deprive it of economic access to the heavy industries of the Ruhr. But it could also mean that Russia would again have to cope with a greater Germany. And among Russians, as well as in the Soviet client states of Eastern Europe, the memory of successive German invasions is still fresh. After Moscow's experience with its Chinese ally, it may prefer to have fewer and not more major powers seated on the rim of the Russian imperium. Nor can the Soviet realm be integrated economically if it relinquishes East German resources.

On the other hand the West Germans are also still suspect among their own allies. The prewar Reich could not be restored without resurrecting the specter of German domination. Current German objectives thus raise critical questions. Will Western Germany try to utilize for her own purposes the world-wide apparatus of power

with which the West, under American leadership, has
warded off the East? She might as long as she has irredentist aims to pursue. As long as she has irredentist
aims, should she have even indirect access to the deterrent? By proposing West German participation in a
mixed-manned multilateral naval unit, the United States
sought to keep German nuclear desires within limits, but
Moscow would have been so embittered by such a NATO
nuclear force, in either its American or British form, the
West could not proceed.

Not that Bonn could, in a NATO Nuclear Force, ever
get a lone German finger on the trigger. But membership
in such a force would enhance Bonn's status and, with
such status, it might step up endeavors to alter the status
quo in Eastern Europe. The preservation of the status
quo in Eastern Europe is what the Russian national interest requires.

France also opposed a NATO Nuclear Force because if
she assigned nuclear weapons to such a project, as Britain
was prepared to assign them, there could be no French
hegemony in Western Europe. So, too, anything that
enhanced the status of West Germany would reduce her
own.

It took courage for postwar France to forgive and
forget. Through NATO, the Bonn Republic was bound
to the West strategically; through the European Communities, especially if there should be a federal merger
to clinch these measures, it would be riveted to the West
economically and governmentally. Russian terms for all-
German reunification might thus be nipped in the bud.
But even if the two Germanies were reunited under
Western auspices, becoming thus a single member of the
West European community, the French would be sub-
merged, as none could withstand a greater Reich in West-

ern Europe, in the Common Market, or in any political union that evolved from it. France might support German reunification as an objective as long as its fulfillment appeared remote; but, in return, France wanted Bonn's assent to realignments within the West through which France supposed her own status would be enhanced. A greater Reich might, in accordance with tradition, play off the East against the West. Already West Germans have had to ride with French hounds and run with American hares. It will not be easy for the United States, as leader of the West, or for the West as a whole, if the Bonn Republic or France, or the two together, try to manipulate a unified Europe for their own purposes.

There are two problems here: that of fitting Western Germany into a unified Europe, and that of fitting a unified Europe into a more concrete Atlantic partnership. These two problems cannot be treated apart.

There is no secret about the roots of the Gaullist mystique, so far as it has been a form of compensation after a degrading Pétainist interlude. And the mystique may have served to remind others that the rank of France cannot be lowered without civilization in general being harmed. But harm can also be done when the swing of the pendulum is too extreme. There has been more to Gaullism than President de Gaulle. As a French phenomenon, or even a European one, it might outlast its author.

Defeat and occupation by the Germans seem to have left less of a scar on official France than the ill will exhibited by her American ally—a recent liberator—during the Suez crisis. A deterrent of her own might now embolden France to talk back openly to Washington.[2] But

2. In general, as a matter of fact, the course that Washington followed during the Suez crisis did much to speed up the formation of the Common Market and the movement toward a "Europe" that would be more detached politically from the United States.

a global balance was what made the French secure as
they extricated themselves from Indochina and North
Africa, let the Fourth Republic be overthrown, and staged
their sit-down strike in NATO.

There could have been no global balance without the
power structure of the West. Yet Gaullist France demanded a drastic transformation in that power structure.
Part of the Gaullist theory has been based on the assumption that America's response to a total nuclear challenge
would be irresolute. The American response during the
Kennedy-Khrushchev encounter over Cuba was unwaver-
ing, but this did not induce General de Gaulle to shift
ground. Instead, he strove even harder for a self-depend-
ent Europe as a substitute for Atlantic interdependence.

France is the best site for much of that NATO machinery through which the North Atlantic Alliance may
be put into effect. Though she has withdrawn from NATO
and has evicted NATO forces from her soil, she still
adheres to the North Atlantic Alliance. As all free peoples
have had a stake in the East-West contest, it has been
more than a struggle between the United States and
Russia. A pox on both your houses has, nevertheless, been
the Gaullist cry.

A higher rank for France within the West is what
General de Gaulle may have wanted most. Resenting
Anglo-American solidarity, he suggested that France com-
bine with the United States and Britain in a sort of
Three Power directorate for the West. But what confi-
dence can the French have inspired in Washington and
London? Who, when the Gaullist era ends, will speak for
France—the Army, moderates of the Center, ultras of the
Right or Left? Most of the NATO capitals would not, in
any case, submit to a NATO directorate, with or without
the French. Still less would they accept the Bonn Re-

public, with France and NATO at loggerheads, as third triumvir for the West.

Even more impracticable would be a directorate of the five nuclear powers. Paris may now be on better terms with Peking and Moscow. Peking, however, is hardly on better terms with either Moscow or the West.

The Gaullist vision of a Europe stretching from the Atlantic to the Urals is both grandiose and naïve. It implies that Russia might relinquish her vast Asian domains. It also implies that a European Third Force, over which the French would preside, can make its own settlement with Russia. But before a Third Force deserted the United States, the United States might desert *it*. A bilateral settlement with Washington is what Moscow, cognizant of global power realities, has long sought. Western Europe should be the last to push the United States into that kind of settlement.

Such were the circumstances in which the United States urged that some room be found for Britain in the new Europe. There was logic in the idea of Britain as a stabilizer. What does have the logic of history against it is, of course, the way France has treated her own Western allies. For this has put fresh emphasis on the place which the West Germans occupy in NATO. It is incredible that that should have been done by the people of Delcassé, the Cambons, Clemenceau and Foch; NATO is the embodiment of much for which they pleaded in vain. And yet here, as far as the British role is concerned, a very clear distinction must be drawn.

It is on German territory that a Russian thrust from Eastern Europe has had to be barred. The Bonn Republic, with its twelve divisions still undermanned, is doing less for its own defense than, in the sphere of conventional weapons and in association with Atlantic allies, it has

undertaken to do. But even if those twelve divisions
give her second place within NATO itself, they do
not make Western Germany the second Power within
the West as a whole. The free world has interests which
extend far beyond the frontiers of the West in Central
Europe. And that brings up the part Britain may still
play. Nowhere can it be a predominant one, but its continuance is as vital as ever.

When disarray in the West is so acute, long-term
trends are what count. There is still much for NATO
to do—and France, as the post-Gaullist French may yet
perceive, still needs its benefits more than most. Though
the Common Market marks time, none of its members
could prosper to the same extent if it was liquidated. The
Common Market cannot do without France; she cannot
do without it. Although France excluded Britain from
the Common Market, Britain must still make up her own
mind whether to seek admission again. The very character
of the Common Market is what has kept France within
it; this, no less, is what should induce Britain to abstain.
For its absorptive capacity may be greater than the British people have been told.

VI FRAMES OF REFERENCE

It can be no simple task to make that unified Europe
which, as the United States has conceived it, may be one
of two equal pillars in the Atlantic edifice. Obscure, too,
will be the nature of the pillar on the North American
side of the Atlantic. Is Canada, for instance, to be in-
cluded? The European pillar is to be cemented by close
integration. But Canada, trying to keep a national identity
of her own, has long resisted closer integration with her
giant American neighbor.

Nor does anybody know where the Latin-American countries will fit in. These countries would be liabilities rather than assets in a hemispherically unified America. While it is true that the United States as well as Europe must do what they can for Latin America, Latin America has little with which to reciprocate, and it is only on a basis of reciprocity that a concrete Atlantic partnership, as advocated by Presidents Kennedy and Johnson, can function.

Not that Latin America should be deemed a peripheral zone. It may be argued that blunders by the United States were what hastened Soviet inroads in the Caribbean. The fact remains that the global balance might have shifted against the West if Russia had been allowed to keep her missiles in Cuba—if the United States had been subjected thenceforth to as direct a threat as her British and West European allies. A paralysis of the over-all American deterrent would have ensued, with Western Europe thus being left as open to Soviet conquest or coercion as Eastern Europe had been. NATO has given most of its attention to the defense of Western Europe. The Cuban crisis, however, exposed the dependence of Western Europe on the hemispheric security of North America as it had never been exposed before.

Such, too, was the angle from which President Johnson's subsequent intervention in the Dominican Republic should have been examined. The information he received from American officials on the spot may or may not have been faulty. Once bitten, twice shy. After Moscow tried to convert Cuba into a Caribbean outpost for Russian missiles, no pro-Soviet regime on another island situated near the North American mainland could be tolerated.

The sudden American reoccupation of the Dominican Republic may have violated the Rio Treaty, the Bogota Charter, and the Charter of the United Nations. But all

these pacts were signed before indirect aggression became a menace—before the East learned how, by estab-
lishing missile bases across the Atlantic, it might put the
heartland of the West "under the gun."

What seemed to be tested, first of all, in the tense,
brief, unheralded confrontation of October, 1962, was
the facility with which the United States could protect
herself. Tested simultaneously was the facility with which
she could, at the same time, uphold the global balance—
and the sequel to that concurrent test, though less dramatic or breath-taking, has been and will be as lasting.

Under an American lead the countervailing defenses
of the West had, since World War II, been penning up
Russia on a world-wide scale. On the same world-wide
scale, Russia would have gained global domination if she
could have broken through those countervailing defenses
in the autumn of 1962. For this was no side adventure on
the periphery of Western power. Russia, under Nikita
Khrushchev, was unable to pull off her planetary coup,
however. No similar opportunity is likely to recur. The
Soviet Union has therefore been constrained to take another course. By 1966, when Alexei Kosygin mediated between India and Pakistan at Tashkent, caution rather than
audacity had become the essence of Russian statecraft.

Two points arise, one negative and one positive. The
accent is on the negative when Europe and America do
not work together. Their rivals in the East labor, provi-
dentially, under even greater disabilities.

When Russia and China trapped weaker neighbors,
they had geography rather than ideology on their side.
But Communist economies will have to do more for their
own people before they can fully mesmerize other developing peoples. Then, too, though Europe and America

might differ over the common defense, the two main sections of the Sino-Soviet camp may yet have to defend themselves against each other. Thus where the West cannot, by its own exertions, save itself, the East, by its dissensions, may help save the West.

Disarray in the East, at any rate, may have a more far-reaching effect than disarray in the West. A common devotion to Marx and Lenin will be of small avail if Peking covets Russian territory and, having gathered under its banner the "have-nots" of Africa, Asia, and Latin America, pits them against Russia as well as the West. For China may thus threaten Russia's national interests—a state of affairs in which power rather than ideology must again be the prime consideration.

The Soviet Union has long employed ideological weapons against the West. It did not, however, foresee a struggle for power with its own Chinese collaborators in which the latter would employ ideological weapons against it. The Soviet Union may even have to take a fresh look at the utility of those weapons in the East-West contest. The Kremlin has put forth its theory of peaceful coexistence—one which presupposed that ideological weapons would enable Russia, if Clausewitz may be rephrased, to pursue power by other, nonmilitary means. But will the pursuit of power against the West by any hostile means always be in the Russian national interest?

Soviet rulers may do all they can to ignore that question. Yet the pressures to which they are subject at home and abroad cannot be ignored. At a time when a better life is within sight for the Russian people, a perpetual crusade against the West should be less and less to its liking. Nor, with Peking to harry Moscow, do the client states of Eastern Europe tend to be as much at Russia's beck and call. The Soviet Union, if only to keep its ideological credentials in good order, might vie with Communist China in subversive activities where it can. These subversive activities may cause Russia to oscillate between reconciliation with the West today and truculence tomorrow. But the circumstances that predispose Russia toward some accommodation with the West cannot, like the cold war itself, be switched on and off. For these circumstances, after all, are less amenable to change.

If, moreover, a détente makes headway, it could acquire a momentum of its own. Like her adversaries in the West, Russia has shunned war lest it get out of control. But peace may get out of control if, despite Moscow's plan for coexistence, all does not go according to plan.

It is, in the end, the vigil maintained by the West that compounds other problems for Russia. Credit must be given to the countervailing global strategy of the West if Russia is persuaded that peaceful coexistence, as she interprets it, is preferable to the cold war, and, as a result, a limited détente proves feasible. But continuing Soviet endeavors to communize others, the illusion that others will assent when Russia wages political warfare as a substitute for war, will not make for a durable peace.

Peaceful coexistence, as Moscow has expounded it, is in fact a slogan for peace that is also a battle cry—a formula for procuring the fruits of war without having to wage war itself.

And until Russia prefers a durable peace to peaceful coexistence, Moscow style, the West will have further use for instruments of persuasion. Some in the West have been tempted, of late, to take these for granted. That, repeating the errors of the 1920's and 1930's, would be premature.

About peace by power there is nothing automatic. Beneficiaries must accordingly still do their share.[1]

The West will stultify itself if its frame of reference is too narrow—if European issues are not put in an Atlantic setting, and if Atlantic issues are not put in a setting that, as with the Commonwealth and Anglo-American friendship, is actually world-wide. It is not astonishing when underprivileged or newly emancipated peoples act confused. For Europeans and North Americans there is less excuse. As long as the West upholds a free-world order, the values of civilized society will be sustained. In upholding those values Europe and America may forge new unities. Old-established ones must also be preserved.

1. An analysis of prewar errors was the starting point for the writer's forecast of postwar realities in *Peace by Power* (New York and London, 1942)—as well as in *The Virginia Quarterly Review*, Spring, 1944.

The postwar transition from a European to a global balance was dealt with in *Reprieve from War* (New York, 1950) and in *America in Britain's Place* (New York and London, 1961).

Minerva may have sprung fully grown from the head of Jupiter, but American policies of "containment" and "positions of strength" had no such dramatic origin. They were simply an adaptation to postwar circumstances of lessons gleaned from prewar errors. Postwar policies, nonetheless, have often been identified with some who were late converts to the concept of peace by power, having opposed it until opposition could no longer pay off.

2

BRITAIN AND EUROPE
Britain Revisited

VII PAST AND PRESENT

Standing on the footbridge that spans the lake in St. James's Park, with Buckingham Palace at one's back, and peering through the trees in the direction of Westminster Abbey, the tower of Big Ben, and the House of Parliament, then glancing toward the offices, roofs, and cupolas of Whitehall—some as gray as London skies, some white with a hint of timeless Oriental magic—one can sense here as well as anywhere the nature of the crisis over her role into which Britain is plunged.

Symbols of the link between past and present, these buildings are no longer command posts in an apparatus for greatness. And yet, as portions of that apparatus remain, where do they fit into any new scheme of things for Britain? Nobody knows. Her entry into the Common Market, as far as it presaged the Europeanization of Britain, would have marked an irreparable break with the past. Was it only by such a break with the past that a viable future could be ensured?

Any such break was averted by edict from the Elysée Palace in Paris and not by decisions made in London at the Palace of Westminster. But why had Britain been exposed to so resounding a snub?

46

Diminished power was the tragic legacy of misjudgment between the wars. If this had not still been exacting its toll, the quest for a closer tie-up with European neighbors might not have been undertaken.

But were issues raised by that quest also misjudged? Britain's entire status might have been recast by entry into the Common Market—with repercussions by which the free world as a whole could be set back. The proceedings at Brussels were enough in themselves to shake the Commonwealth relationship. Other damage might also have been wrought. Certainly Britain's margin for error is slimmer than it once was. Does she repel would-be conquerors only to defeat herself?

The neat, placid charm of St. James's Park should not ordinarily elicit forebodings as dour as these. They are, however, less keen than those one felt on this spot (though the footbridge is new) during the 1930's—for, after all, nothing done at Westminster will again matter so much.

But it still does matter a good deal—otherwise, why worry? For letting war recur, Britain made amends during the war itself. But did one, after a long absence, perceive analogies between the atmosphere of prewar Britain and of Britain today? The issues are not the same. And yet, when one delves into them, old unhappy far-off things unhappily seem less far off.

VIII THE BRITISH MOOD

Britain could never have applied for membership in the Common Market in 1961 if she had not, unwitting and taciturn, undergone an epoch-making change of outlook. And while she will not be joining it just now, that change

began with others that leave their stamp. An economic
lag brought this development to a head; many interrelated segments of British life were no less sluggish. The
subjects under discussion were wages, salaries, profits,
dividends, national productivity, exports, and the balance
of payments. But urgency was also lent to Britain's great
debate by changes in the markets of the world, by the
massive postwar expansion of the American economy,
by the economic upsurge of the new Europe. The British
people had to have a better footing among those changes
if, with the passing of primacy, their decline were to be
arrested. An economic crisis for Britain was thus more
than economic.

It was argued that by joining the Common Market
the scale of output among major British industries might
be expanded and a larger amount of research undertaken.
This would enable British industries to offer manufactured
goods that were more up to date. In that way, the argument continued, capital might be kept at home while
Britain could attract American and other foreign invest-
ments that European neighbors had been getting. But
farming in Britain would no longer be protected from
European agriculture and, as Commonwealth trade agreements were dropped, advantages gained from them also
would be wiped out; new taxes on overseas foodstuffs
would raise the cost of living and render British exports
less competitive than ever. Yet proponents of British
membership in the Common Market did not want only to
have British industry braced, as it must be, for competition. Once Britain had girded herself for such competition,
she would exercise more authority in other spheres.

The method chosen, however, must not be one which
caused Britain to lose her political identity. That, nevertheless, is what might happen if an unexamined fatalism

—the notion that in an age of giant technologies Britain must become an integral part of a bigger continental economy—sapped her will.

Britain is unable to duplicate the conditions under which every type of electronic computer and long-range aircraft may be produced successfully. But why should she have to do so if there are still types of goods that, with an effort, she can still manufacture efficiently, and forms of service—like that which the City of London offers the world—that she can still render best?

Various countries may tend more and more to belong to larger groupings, old and new, loose and tight, continental and extracontinental. Yet groupings that sell must also buy. None can live unto themselves alone.

While it is true that Britain lags economically, this has not been due to the fact that the United States today and Western Europe tomorrow may produce computers more cheaply. And even if Britain could overcome an economic lag by joining the Common Market, the cost in other respects might be prohibitive.

Perhaps Britain had to negotiate for membership before the nation could get the price of entry into its head. But in some British quarters membership was welcomed as an end in itself and without full regard for its political consequences. How did this state of mind arise? To what can it be ascribed?

Old laurels wilt rapidly and the British people have had scant relish for winning new ones of late. While glitter and glamour attest to outward recovery from the stress of war, one does not have to scratch far below the surface for evidence of strain (after years of depression, heavy taxation, postwar austerity) and social tensions, both old and new.

A bent toward insularity, for which the British people

were once renowned, might be suppressed as long as
Britain operates on a broad global front. But it could re-
vive and reclaim its own. Withdrawal from without has
been accompanied by withdrawal from within. Political
disengagement abroad and moral disengagement at home
have kept pace with each other. And this mood has also
been aided by devices of mass entertainment that are so
apt everywhere to induce mass torpor.

Then, too, full employment and the Welfare State
have fostered tendencies to sink back and turn inward.
Britain cannot deliver the goods if she is plagued by
slackness and unauthorized strikes not only in her factories but at her ports.[1] Full employment, as a matter of
fact, has been less than full among the old heavy industries above the Mersey and Humber. Elsewhere, however,
the problem may have been one not only of full employment but of "over-full employment." Whatever has fostered demands for wage increases and thus raised costs
has made British goods less competitive abroad when
they should be more competitive. And now, after a
euphoric period of lopsided affluence, the trade and monetary crisis by which Britain has been assailed seems like
a bad dream. It is, alas, no bad dream but a mortifying
actuality.

Deflation sets in as Britain adopts measures that might
enable her, over the years, to repay foreign banks that
have come to her rescue. Unemployment may be kept
within bounds. Will the mood of the British people alter
if the bite of deflation is a comparatively gentle one; if,
after "over-full employment" has been reduced, full em-

1. Many British port facilities are out of date and tight little monopolies
govern the work of stevedores, dockers, and lightermen. In the Middle
Ages, one Scandinavian newspaper is reported to have observed, it took
five days to send a cargo ship from England to France. Today, on the
average, it takes three weeks.

ployment continues? It is too soon to say. Adversity has brought out the best in the British people in the past. But this will be of no avail if they again take the wrong path.

IX PREREQUISITES FOR BRITAIN

Britain can no longer play as great a part in world affairs as she once did. An important role as European stabilizer has, all the same, been contemplated for her. But what if the Common Market is converted into a federal union? Could the stabilizing role of a British component then be effective? It would be less and not more effective than it has been.

It was as the hub of an oceanic complex that a small Britannic island in the North Sea once played a part beyond its own intrinsic power—and this part was sustained by overseas affinities to which no single federated unit might individually cling. Ontario and Massachusetts cannot possess external ties of their own. Neither could Britain possess any if, exchanging sovereign rights for provincial ones, she joined political Europe as a state of the union.[1]

An integrated Britain might, to be sure, maintain overseas affinities as long as there was a Gaullist ban on an outright fusion—on a federal merger that would make Western Europe, as it made the United States, one and indivisible. But how long would that ban last?

As a federated unit Britain could not serve as pivot of a world-wide Commonwealth and, without its British

---

1. There are some in the Province of Quebec who would like to violate that rule. If they do, the Canadian Confederation will have been made unworkable and Canada will have been rent asunder.

pivot, the Commonwealth would break up. Was an integrated Britain worth more than historic moorings by which the free world had long been steadied? Those moorings, despite all that has changed, are still an inestimable boon. Could Britain relinquish overseas sources of strength and still have leverage in European affairs? Some among the British knew that she could not, that her status would be jeopardized. Why were so few prepared at first to face the facts?

X PORTENTS

The effect of Europeanization on Britain's status should have been the nub of Britain's great debate, and yet that is the one point about which the least has been said. The way in which awkward features of so vital a topic could be kept in the shade will be suggested later on, but why it was done is germane at this juncture.

It was in keeping with the mood of the British people that an easy way out should have been sought. And only when the allies of Britain indicated that they might compel her to make choices that she should not have been compelled to make was sufficient heed paid to what had always been the basic realities.

Was membership in the Common Market the only solution? What if the British people were summoned to a drastic Churchillian effort at national self-regeneration? Belatedly, some belt-tightening *has* taken place, but for heroic measures the British people have been far from ready.

And if that is so, does it not explain the lack of candor among the majority of opinion-makers and opinion media at the time of the British bid for entry into the Common

Market? When the public was left undisturbed, it was given what it wanted. But the diffidence of the Establishment has been a portent. For Britain is the only major country of the West whose status has rested on overseas props. How much do the British people now care about these?

There could be no turning toward Europe that did not signify a turning away from those with whom Britain, in her days of pre-eminence, had been most closely affiliated. And such bonds could never have been downgraded if the British people, with conviction, still wished to play an important part in the world—even in Europe itself. Britain, however, could not deviate from the world-wide to the regional without the entire range of policy being correspondingly reduced.

There may yet be time for Britain to avert so momentous a diversion. But an element of escapism must first be dispelled. Here, at any rate, is where resemblances between a contemporary impulse and the self-destructive tone of the 1930's is bound to strike the observer. For when appeasers (with their counterparts among the isolationists of the United States and Canada) misjudged issues then, they had wide popular backing. Friends were deemed enemies and enemies deemed friends. It was believed that the French rather than the Germans had been the chief miscreants over the years; that any warlike German designs were aimed solely against Russia, and that the West did not therefore have to combine and rearm; that the way to do justice was to discourage allies in Western Europe and to forsake countries in Central Europe which should never have been forsaken. The European balance of power was an historic staple of British policy that should never have been ignored. Ignored it was.

There may be no exact analogy between prewar Britain, with her self-defeating irrationalities, and the problems of Britain today. But if Britain had not evaded first principles between the wars, she might not have had to fight again for her life. Now, with a lessened capacity, she may still have a contribution to make. But how well can she make it if yet another set of fundamentals has been evaded?

XI SCHISM IN THE COMMONWEALTH?

The attitude of Europeanizers toward Commonwealth ties and Anglo-American friendship has necessarily been ambivalent. Not that these classic vehicles were deemed expendable at once. They had, on the contrary, to be conserved and put to use if the capitals of the Common Market drove too hard a bargain. But how would the British have treated these vehicles if some accord had been attained and bets no longer hedged? Now or later Britain may shrink from a political and social contract through which she would be utterly Europeanized. But she might have contracted out of traditional bonds long before that point had been reached.

The Commonwealth is, *par excellence*, the product of a more sanguine era. In recent times many members have openly quarreled with Britain at the United Nations. There has been doubt whether Commonwealth partners can promise Britain as big an expansion in trade as the Common Market could furnish. In Britain, moreover, the complaint has been voiced that Commonwealth burdens are disproportionate. And it is true that overseas countries, including the United States in her formative years, were sheltered by the *Pax Britannica* when it held sway.

Afterward, nevertheless, Britain's role as a pivot of the Commonwealth bolstered her own rank in world affairs and did much to uphold her modern status. Britain may have done more for the Commonwealth entity in peacetime than Commonwealth partners have done for Britain. It is an entity, however, in which óthers still converge upon Britain or revolve around her. And, as long as they do that, the British stake in the Commonwealth will be the largest of all.

Then, too, intangibles as well as tangibles have entered into the reckoning. Where these lent prestige and influence, they were, in themselves, an element of power. But they were also something more—and because of them the Commonwealth account has been less top-heavy than has often been averred.

A materialist interpretation of history must exclude from its credo great imponderables such as those that impelled many volunteers from across the seas to rally to Britain's side when she was up against it in two world wars. The struggle for equality of status among other Commonwealth countries never altogether blotted out a moral investment in Britain which is still cherished by a numerous host and for which neither Marx nor Mammon provided. To Britain's own younger generation, however, all this means little. An affection that is not felt cannot be requited. In the indifference of the British, moreover, there has been a wry logic. They no longer have strength to take the lead. Overseas sources of strength therefore do not rate high.

This is not to say there has been more devotion in other Commonwealth countries to the Commonwealth bond. It is to say that Britain does not give without also getting. Yet the Left seems more conscious of these questions nowadays than the Right or Center. Between them, as a matter of fact, there has been an historic transposition. The *volte face* has been one by which a prewar observer of British public life might well be astounded.

The Empire was long a stock in trade for the Right. Others worked out the idea of the Commonwealth before it caught the imagination of the Left. But Asian and African countries have of late formed a majority among members of the Commonwealth. Most have had a neutralist and anticolonial outlook. There has, however, been more to the Commonwealth than just its new African members. As modern states, they have barely been set going. Their backwardness, all the same, is what many Europeanizers have first singled out as the most typical feature of the Commonwealth as a whole. There will be less point to that argument if some African members, out of impatience with British policy in Rhodesia, secede.

There also has been disillusion in Britain with "white" overseas countries of the Commonwealth. It is remarkable, nevertheless, that terms of entry into the Common Market which would split the Commonwealth should be opposed more insistently by the Labour Party than by the Conservative Party.

Europeanizers have defined the issue as a choice primarily between Europe and the Commonwealth. That is a false antithesis. There can be nothing mutually exclusive between the varied sources of British strength. Britain needs them all. Such is the issue. And only if it is treated as one that towers above party loyalties are wider interests, national and international, sure to be put first.

Much in Britain's status depends on her capacity to attract others. And "Europe" cannot become a magnet for Britain without Britain herself ceasing to be a magnet. Her entry into the Common Market has been discussed mostly as an economic problem. But it is the politics of the Common Market which, if she joined that body, would decide her fate.

XII PLAYED OUT OR PLAYED DOWN?

The Commonwealth is not the only traditional source of British strength that could be impaired by whatever Europeanized the British people unduly. Another factor enabling Britain to play a part beyond her physical power has been Anglo-American friendship. As recently as the 1940's, when all else had crumbled, this factor (together with support for Churchill's Britain from other Commonwealth countries) constituted a still unappreciated mainstay for civilized society.

Britain, however, was no longer first in an Anglo-American combine and, even if co-operation with the United States were less irksome, that alone might have dispirited many Britons. Some would have voluntarily soft-pedaled Britain's role as prime mover of the Commonwealth; what still troubled others was that her role as Anglo-American prime mover had passed from her involuntarily. But the overseas interests of Britain had long impinged on each other. Whatever made her swerve from Commonwealth links would also make her swerve from those with the United States.

All the same, one difference can be noted. Commonwealth partners could not be let down without a feeling of guilt. A chance to veer away from the United States might have been greeted in a few British quarters with relief. And special pleaders made light of any special relationship. For in this context, as in others, there were revisionists who hoped to reshape history by rewriting it.

Was a separate British role, one based on Common-

wealth and Anglo-American ties, "about played out?"
Many were incensed when Dean Acheson, a former
American Secretary of State, alleged that it was. But
among those who rebuked him for saying this were some
who had themselves been playing it down.

General de Gaulle, on the other hand, perceived that
this role had not been played out. He opposed Britain's
entry into the Common Market because it could in fact
be performed. But if Britain kept traditional bonds—and
a Gaullist union of states would have permitted members
to do that—she would have retained access to exterior
sources of strength, to the means for checking a nascent
French hegemony. General de Gaulle did not want to be
checked. This was not the first time that a European
statesman, paying an inadvertent tribute to Commonwealth ties and Anglo-American friendship, had appraised
these two factors—elusive, ill-defined, mostly latent, singu-
larly efficacious—better than the English-speaking peoples
themselves. President de Gaulle may have been a hostile
witness, but he did not, as a rule, tilt at windmills.

Paradox abounded. Discontent over American leadership provided one impetus for Europeanizing trends in
Britain. But in any event it had been an American aim to
spur on these Europeanizing trends. There would be less
risk of any Third Force or anti-American aberrations if
Britain belonged to a united Europe. Washington thus
set store by Anglo-American friendship—though this very
factor would fade away if a tight-knit European union, as
endorsed by the United States, severed a British component from overseas bonds. Washington wished to keep
a veto on the use of nuclear weapons. At the same time
American nuclear secrets entrusted to Britain could not
be withheld from France if the British and French, with
American blessings, were integrated politically. So, too,

some Europeanizers among the British presupposed that the primacy of Western Europe lay within their grasp— as though the French and West Germans, who had the upper hand, would concur. And as though, after world- wide links had been attenuated, Britain would have more rather than less strength for making a bid of that sort.

But in spite of all this, the Commonwealth is one of the great political achievements of modern times and even Europeanizers did not want it scrapped if it could some- how be salvaged. The suggestion was made therefore that the United States should replace Britain as its center. Europeanizers may have minimized the connection be- tween overseas bonds and Britain's role in Europe; they did, nevertheless, recognize that overseas bonds, Com- monwealth and Anglo-American, have had an intercon- nection of their own. And yet any suggestion that the United States might replace Britain as center of the Commonwealth was a nonstarter for three insuperable reasons:

1. The first was that, while the perpetuation of the Commonwealth is a major American interest, it can never be the same as Britain's own stake in the Commonwealth.

2. The second was that overseas members would not accept the suggestion. There are countries that have se- ceded without the Commonwealth dissolving. If Britain secedes (the one eventuality that, prior to the Common Market campaign, had not been foreseen), the Common- wealth will dissolve as a group and there will be nothing left to hand over.

Like Britain, a number of overseas Commonwealth countries have ties of their own with the United States. But these, in genesis and character, are not the same as those out of which the Commonwealth evolved.

3. And that brought up another inherent obstacle.

The Commonwealth took its rise from the British political
system, and the British political system is what enabled
Britain to serve as its pivot. There is little in the American
political system that would provide for a similar role.

Must Britain, in charting a new course, desert well-
trodden ones? Commonwealth and American paths were
often rocky, but they had long been mapped out. Now
Britain might have unknown spheres to traverse. The
political traditions of European traveling companions may
be more alien than those of former associates. The new
bonds would have to be closer, permanent, immutable.

And so the springs from which misjudgment might
again flow have, as during the epoch of isolationism and
appeasement, been many and diverse. Britain's status
rests on historic prerequisites. These have been misconceived in the United States. But some among the British,
so as to rationalize their own preference for Europe, have
also misconceived those prerequisites.

XIII A REDISCOVERY OF EUROPE

Many have contended that in negotiating for entry into
the Common Market Britain only bowed to the inevitable—and while the inevitable might be postponed it
cannot be put off indefinitely. But a retreat is not an
advance—and the fact that it could be presented as one
may be a clue to much in postwar Britain that transcends
this particular episode.

Would Britain have allayed one set of frustrations by
inviting others still more frustrating? When the emphasis
shifts from the world-wide to the European, there is a
narrowing of horizons. Impulses that have been half-

forgotten and long repressed may, as a result, be given a chance to reassert themselves.

An outer island province of Western Europe cannot persist as hub of an oceanic complex, but it might hark back to its own origins—to roots that are Norman, if not Roman. For the English, after all, the Age of Discovery coincided with the loss of their last footholds across the Channel. The legacy of that age is precisely what Britain today, in one way or another, has been writing off or writing down. Not that she ever ceased to be a European Power in the spheres of war and diplomacy. But another fabric with tighter strands is also being rewoven and this task has been assisted by a rediscovery of Europe itself.

It has been a rediscovery, moreover, in which, since the advent of the Welfare State, all classes could take part. Never before have so many British workers enjoyed holidays in European countries: the Grand Tour has been made over into a mass phenomenon by cheap travel and full employment. Though language barriers still divide, the folkways of European neighbors will, all the same, soon appear less strange than those of more distant English-speaking associates.

This rediscovery of Europe is no transient phase. As it has come to stay, it made things easier for Harold Macmillan when negotiations were first undertaken for Britain's entry into the Common Market. And if Britain's place in history is affected by what he tried to do—or what he left for his political disciples to do—what place in history will he occupy? All that can be said as yet is that he would not have wanted to be known as the one who blazed a trail that wound up in a blind alley. The mantle of Charlemagne is for those who have been in the van rather than the rear of European unification. But a Euro-

peanized status for Britain would resemble that which
she held during the Middle Ages. Will the British people
retrace steps that the Normans took? They might. A
British statesman, however, would have to impose his
will on other nations before he could figure as some
William the Conqueror in reverse. And unless pressure
for organic union could be withstood, it is Britain that,
on being Europeanized, would lose out.

XIV THE CONDITIONS OF DEBATE

Those who proposed Britain's entry into the Common
Market raised the most subtle of political issues without
ever admitting its subtlety. But not all the British people
could be misled. The change of outlook among them was,
as it were, a reorientation of the disoriented. Since
World War II they had been taking refuge in apathy,
insularity, and a somewhat plaintive yearning for the
quiet life—a mood to which, during the Common Market
campaign, many among the chief opinion media seemed
blandly attuned. From Brussels, however, came a por-
trait of Britain as suppliant and this stirred unease in a
great, proud nation whose seasoned political instincts
were dormant but not dead. The official Left in Britain
thereupon descended from its perch on the fence and
lined up with other skeptics.

The Beaverbrook press did, of course, storm against
British entry into the Common Market. Its more sedate
rivals purveyed soothing syrup, and almost no forum ex-
isted for a middle view. There were exceptions. The
blackout was not as complete as that devised by the
British press and the British Broadcasting Corporation
over the romance that cost Edward VIII his throne.

Those were the years of appeasement when opinion media, led by *The Times,* did much to demoralize Britain and thus undo the West. Was a Nazi-Soviet pact, expediting German ascendancy, the logical outcome to British imprescience? It was only by the skin of one's teeth that one managed to get an early warning of that danger published.[1]

And as then, so now—can the British public be made aware of what membership in the Common Market might entail? Major opinion media seem more eager to manipulate than to clarify or enlighten. And this cannot occur without a prewar observer of the British scene feeling this is where he came in—a sensation of watching a repeat performance at another turning point for Britain and the West.

There is more to haunt him, however, than some recollection, faint and fleeting, of *déjà vu,* of here we go

1. The writer's warning of a Nazi-Soviet Pact appeared in *The Fortnightly* (London), March, 1938—a year and a half before the event, six months before Munich, two weeks before the fall of Austria. The article made the point that there might be a Russo-German agreement that would divide up Poland and put the West at Germany's mercy if Austria were to go under and the independence of Czechoslovakia were thereby undermined.

Neither the Left nor the Right was disposed to give that sort of power analysis a hearing. The Left would not believe that Stalin might do business with Hitler, and the Right would not believe that Hitler might do business with Stalin.

In this analysis the writer also pointed out that the United States needed Britain to maintain a European balance with which the world distribution of power was bound up. Such a balance upheld "an international order" in which democracies could survive. In "any final crisis" the same view of human society would draw Britain and the United States together.

Perhaps the writer may also recall here how, some months before the fall of Austria, *The News Chronicle,* a London newspaper, published an article by him on German sabotage in America during World War I and how he had tried to suggest that Papen, the Nazi Ambassador at Vienna, was then doing in Austria what he had once done in the United States. It was typical of the time (November 12, 1937) that an editorial blue pencil should have removed from the published article so topical a reference to Papen.

again. When opinion media behaved as they did, when foreclosures on dissent were taken for granted, one could not help asking whether the conditions of public debate were as free as the British people thought them to be. They presumed that these were better in Britain than in the United States. But were they?

When bigness prevails, large-scale opinion media are still free to compete with each other. What makes them instruments of conformity is that fewer and fewer have more and more capacity to penetrate every nook and cranny of the social order. The British supposedly excel Americans on the score of individuality. But while Britons may not conform in the same way as Americans, they conform at least as much in their own individual way.

And they do not do so simply at the behest of the nation's ingrown power elite, the so-called Establishment. Against it there are rival coteries, anti-Establishment Establishments, that have the same joint capacity to put across their own preconceived ideas on an ever-enlarged scale. Meanwhile, there may be less and less room for unorganized dissent.

As in the United States, so in Britain, a clash of opposing group conformities, Left, Right and Center, is what maintains political freedom, while freedom of expression might be more constricted than it has been for the unaffiliated individual.

It may be that British libel laws have been too harsh. But they do not hamper in spheres where British opinion media are prone to manipulate. Some British opinion media played tricks with the public during the Vassal spy case; most of them (apart from mercenary scandal sheets) acted as watchdogs of the public interest during the Profumo affair of 1963. In sensational episodes such as these, nevertheless, self-interest (so far as circulation figures were boosted and radio-TV audiences enlarged) was also promoted. But over such issues as Britain's entry into the Common Market, or the strategic background to the Kennedy-Khrushchev tussle over Soviet missile bases in Cuba, British opinion media were more erratic.

Nor did many give a full picture when the Republican Party nominated Senator Barry Goldwater for the American Presidency. As fears of American unpredictability revived, some influential British opinion media reiterated their view that Britain's future lay mainly in Europe.

Not that there is any dearth of solicitude for the right of the British people to hear all sides. More and more, however, the information they get comes through media with information axes of their own to grind. And in this respect they may prove even worse off than Americans. For geography has ordained one salient difference in conditions of debate between English-speaking democracies. Although concentration of control has long typified the American economy its opinion media operate across a continental expanse, and public opinion is therefore more difficult to manipulate. But opinion media in Britain are less dispersed physically.

The British Broadcasting Corporation, for instance, is publicly owned and its serious programs have surpassed those that American counterparts have produced. Contrariwise, no single American network has as much of this formative opinion-making field to itself—dividends being the main concern of privately owned British television companies. Excessive commercialism may debase American taste. And yet in Britain there may be an erosion of free debate—one that is intrusive, unremitting, and unobserved—because a high-minded near-monopoly is less open-minded than it pretends to be. The British public cannot always tell where there have been abuses of power.[2] Only the more flagrant ones can usually be detected.

Conditions of debate, then, may not be exactly the same in Britain as in the United States. Bigness, nevertheless, has furnished the same techniques of manipulation. And for these techniques a façade of open-mindedness is required. British and American opinion media permit writers and speakers to range, at full length, upon less decisive questions. As a result, the extent to which another sort of treatment is reserved for more crucial topics may seldom be suspected. To have these crucial topics handled by staff members is to ensure that a desired line will be imposed.

It is assumed in free societies that independent views can always obtain access to the general public. But there is less access when issues arise that cut to the bone. Access is withheld, in other words, when it is most needed.

Not that such foreclosures on dissent are the same as the ideological conditioning in which totalitarian countries engage. The masses cannot be regimented, after all, as long as a small number of large-scale media may still vie with each other. Yet when bigness takes over, matters are discussed less and less on their merits. And this is so among all types of opinion media—among those that have liberal values as a stock in trade as much as any.

The quest for power through manipulation is as intense on the Left and at the Center as on the Right. And open-mindedness is one of its casualties. Opinion

2. During the Common Market campaign, when Britain's overseas connections were being played down, there were two BBC talks on Anglo-American friendship and both depicted that factor as an unhistorical myth. But truth is a myth for those who have myths of their own to purvey.

media may serve liberal causes, but an illiberal liberalism is often manifest behind the scenes. This is not a feature of bigness that should be dismissed lightly. For even as they combat one kind of reaction, illiberal liberals may pave the way for another.

In behavior, opinion media on the Left, Right, and Center are much the same. Few are apt to play fairly when they are playing for keeps.

The English-speaking peoples would not let a fully directed society take hold. And yet a partial dirigism creeps in when the public is denied information to which it is entitled, or when there are unofficial controls over the exchange of opinion. "Evil communications," according to St. Paul, "corrupt good manners." Most opinion media seek, in their own fashion, to oppose evil. But in the sphere of opinion, communication can be free only when it is many-sided. It cannot be many-sided when other objectives come first.

Here, at any rate, is a problem for democracy in Britain with which previous generations did not have to cope. And it is one of which not all are unaware. Are those apprised of arbitrary rulings disposed to resist? Democracy is devitalized when it cannot pass that test. In Britain today it does not pass that test with flying colors. What has been concluded instead is that nothing can be done about such abuses of power, that against them there is virtually no appeal. Yet would acquiescence of that sort have been conceivable if the spirit of the British people had not changed? Europeanism has been one sign of an altered outlook. Another set of changes has also been at work.

XV   A NEW ETHIC

"You can't fight City Hall" is the immortal American
phrase with which the weak and disinherited back away
from an unequal contest with overweening authority. But
the futility of protest is not all that accounts for a sub-
missiveness so inconsistent with the genius of British
history. A fitful new ethic—one which discards objective
standards as yardsticks and decides matters by more sub-
jective criteria—is widespread. Respect for the individual,
a predilection for hearing all sides, sprang from a code
of fair play for which the Victorians and Edwardians, at
their best, were celebrated. At odds with it is a new vein
of sentimentality.

That new vein of sentimentality should not be confused with more familiar British types. There is one, a
sort of vulgarized mass loyalism, which must embarrass
occupants of the Throne and members of the Royal Fam-
ily. There is another, a pacifist streak personified by
George Lansbury before World War II and by Bertrand
Russell in the nuclear age, which derives from an authen-
tic, if misguided, idealism. This new trait does not stem
from idealism, however, but from the instinct for self-
preservation as adapted to a large-scale economy.

It is the tacit ganging up of job holders who deem
themselves threatened when fault is found with one of
their kind. "There, but for the grace of God, go I," is the
spirit in which sympathy is collectivized. It is also the
spirit in which conformity is reinforced even among
some who profess to spurn it.

Correctives against the grosser varieties of social in-
justice have been embodied in the Welfare State. Yet
this is far from utopia and whatever assuages one sort of

insecurity may excite another. The insecure may even resent those who would assess public questions on their merits as they have other priorities. Nor will they be intent upon protecting democracy against manipulation. With their own brand of herd cynicism they, too, would manipulate if they got the chance.

There is still complacency among the British, but it has its ups and downs. "I'm all right, Jack" is a boast that may be heard less often as economic insecurity returns, as some unemployment results from measures taken to make Britain solvent again. The numbers of the insecure have, moreover, been swollen by those of the upper and middle classes who have come down in the world. As the British outlook alters, so may the things about which feathers can be ruffled. Only a people scarred by what they have been through and still apprehensive could, at bottom, still be so fretful.

Simultaneous with change in the character of British society has been change in the British character—and that also may have some bearing on the British role. It is in the light of customary values that the masses are inert and self-engrossed. Where more recent values are touched, they may close ranks and react with vehemence. But then values have been reshuffled among others, too. Not all gentlemen have had titles and all who possess titles are not necessarily gentlemen. Yet during the 1930's, as one recalls them, there were still rules of the game that only cads and bounders would violate. The 1960's have a more egalitarian, less chivalric code, and though cads and bounders as a species may not be extinct, the very use of these epithets has died out.

If sentimentality was the morality of the insecure, a crowning virtue of the secure was magnanimity. As a quality that a secure aristocratic order could best reveal, it earned praise from Burke and Churchill. Its passing has been lamented. But it could not hope to outlast the state of affairs by which it was bred. At any rate, a people that could afford to be magnanimous could also afford, when things at home or abroad went amiss, to be open-minded about its own imperfections. But magnanimity waned when the British were less sure of themselves, and they were less open-minded when magnanimity waned.

Europeanization would restrict Britain's scope. Is this likely to put her in a more buoyant, self-confident mood? The emotions of the British people have not always been disguised by a calm and phlegmatic exterior; decorum, reticence, and imperturbable good form had a Victorian— Arnold of Rugby—as their apostle. Over the centuries, however, poetry, science, fruits of the creative imagination have testified to much in the British temperament that has been introspective, feminine in intuitiveness, highly strung. Britain won her spurs when these sensibilities commingled with an extrovert practicality in law, politics, defense, invention, industry, commerce, and finance. A seafaring tradition was not all that made Britain the hub of an oceanic complex. And there were outlets for gifts of every description when she had a global theater in which talent could be expressed, energies harnessed, and even inner hostilities dissipated as between man and man and man and society.

But what outlets would Britain have, what could her demeanor be when, secluded from new associates linguistically, she had only a smaller, crowded European stage on which to act? She would have fewer outlets, her demeanor would scarcely be sweetened. And insularity would not be curbed if she was still psychologically islanded off.

XVI POWER AND WILL POWER

Europeans themselves impeded the Europeanization of Britain when entry into the Common Market was blocked. And there was irony in the fact that the other major countries of Western Europe could set terms for one of their own chief liberators. They would seem to have recovered more thoroughly than Britain from the ordeal of World War II. Each had received American economic aid. Nature, moreover, had been kind to France, helping her to recover economically from World War II before she had recovered politically from the French Revolution. Without reserves of brute strength the Germans, like the Russians, could never have done what they have done in both peace and war.

Britain, by way of contrast, had to bank on skill in mustering resources that were always far-flung and often impalpable. Will power did most to see her through the trials and tribulations of World War II. But will power may ebb and what this has held together might fall apart when there is infirmity of will.

Would Britain, by lowering her sights, make things harder and not easier for herself? She did that before. During the era of appeasement, when she was her own worst enemy, others had to be pro-British in spite of the British. They were so not because Britain's record was unsullied, but because she was still the principal guarantor of civilized society. Then, at a decisive juncture, Britain could uphold civilized society only by being upheld. Her function tomorrow will not be what it was yesterday but, within limits, there is still much for her to do. It cannot be done if what must first be reaffirmed is renounced.

XVII THE ISSUE RESTATED

"Look to your moat." That, said Halifax at the end of the seventeenth century, was what Englishmen must do to be saved in this world. It is, nevertheless, by filling in the storied moat that some Britons nowadays would attain economic and political salvation. "The first article of an Englishman's political creed must be," according to Halifax, "that he believeth in the sea." But how can belief in the sea be the first article of an Englishman's political creed when the British Isles, with the emphasis shifting from oceanic to European ties, may become a mere adjunct of Continental land power?

It has been argued that in the second half of the twentieth century some other article of faith is needed. But a more cogent formula has yet to be broached. Britain has long had one foot planted in Europe and another planted across the seas. Europe cannot now offer her, nor can she now offer Europe, a better stance.

Britain's lesser world role was the outcome of misjudgment between the wars. Will postwar misjudgment lessen it still further? This question would not have arisen, or, having risen, could have been answered with more assurance, if the British public and the British opinion-makers were more disposed to come to grips with basic realities. Has a continental formula for the salvation of Britain been an invalid one? If it has, then wisdom may still reside in a more ancient political creed. But it will do so only if the British people take themselves in hand. Will they?

Britain's Great Debate

XVIII THE DYNAMICS OF INTEGRATION

The British Empire, in Seeley's famous phrase, was acquired in a fit of absence of mind. By the same token, will it be in a fit of absence of mind that Britain veers away from the overseas world toward Europe? A number of major questions still call for an answer.

To what extent, for example, could the political consequences of close economic integration with European neighbors be kept within bounds? Federation, it is true, is not yet an item on the European agenda; *à l'anglais mais sans les Anglais*—that was the sort of European unity President de Gaulle envisaged. But the Common Market would have to be liquidated before the economic unification of Western Europe could be stopped. And that would be a misfortune from which, as General de Gaulle laid down the law, all its members shrank. There may, for the moment, be little more institutional progress. There is progress, nevertheless, as long as myriad exchanges link members of the Common Market in an ever-tightening economic unity day by day. For it is on such economic unity that, sooner or later, the completed edifice must repose.

Those who espouse a partial federation would do well to recollect how the United States first tried one in the

eighteenth century without avail. What also may remembered are the successive stages, including a loose customs
union, through which Bismarck finally unified the German Reich. The ground was cleared for the man of blood
and iron by the mild, prosaic Zollverein.

Integration grows by what it feeds on—a lesson to be
drawn from the modern experience of the American
economy. It was assumed that Britain could extricate herself at will from the process of integration and the federalizing trends that this would bring into play. A political
union is to follow the Treaty of Rome by which the
Common Market was established in 1957. But obligations
incurred under it, unlike those prescribed by the Treaty
of Rome itself, may not be specifically irrevocable.

There is more to be considered, however, than the
presumed efficacy of legal safeguards. For these cannot
bottle up dynamic, all-absorbing impulses that could
transform the British economy once the threshold of the
Common Market is crossed. Would Britain ever desire to
switch into reverse? To do so she would have to retain
economic controls that, as she is integrated with others,
would be slipping progressively from her grasp.

The French veto on British membership in 1963 re-
tarded this process of integration. A Gaullist brake would
have slowed it up temporarily even if Britain had joined.
As a sop to her partners, Gaullist France permitted a
liaison, through the Western European Union, to be
maintained between Britain and the Common Market.
Nothing came of it. Nothing could.

Paris and London shared the belief that the growth
of supranational authority could be arrested. And yet at
first, in arresting its growth, the Gaullist French were not
prepared to work with the British. Their other European
aims stood in the way. But, with the departure of General

de Gaulle, these may alter. What does not alter are pre-requisites for Britain—the degree to which her sources of strength must still be diverse. It will, in the last resort, be British and not French interests that rule out the Euro-peanization of Britain.

XIX BRITISH INFLUENCE?

It has been argued in these pages that in the new Europe legal safeguards cannot stave off forever an all-out federal involvement. Britain would have introduced such legal safeguards had she joined the Common Market and as a political union emerged. What long-range support could she have expected?

General de Gaulle did not welcome a British presence, and a post-Gaullist regime which might be more federalist in aspiration will not make things cosier for Britain. Be-sides, Britain's principal European backers are the most ardent of European federalizers. In their own interest the weaker members of the European Communities will sup-port Britain when she acts as a foil to the French and the West Germans. That is why they would have her join. Their federalizing aims may have been put in cold storage so as to speed the entry of Britain into the Com-mon Market. But would these aims be withheld when Britain herself needed support for resisting a fuller integration?

Here, then, is another issue which demands further scrutiny. The British were assured that an integrated Britain would exert great influence across the English Channel. That, however, may be easier said than done. Superior political gifts would, it was whispered, carry the day. And yet without something more substantial,

as the Brussels negotiations were to make plain, a fair
bargain could not readily be struck with the Common
Market itself.

Associate membership, on the other hand, would enable Britain to gain some economic advantages without
being federalized, without forfeiting Commonwealth and
Anglo-American ties. But a unified Europe will have its
inner political sanctum. An associate member, shut out
from this, cannot run the show. Associate membership is
a solution against which Europeanizers in Britain have
long fought shy.

A desire to run the show, of course, could never be
blazoned forth. That would be diplomatically indiscreet.
But, in Britain's great debate, there has been no such
reticence about another feature of the same problem.
Yet it, too, calls for more clarification than it has had.

In world politics, we are told, there will be seats at
the top table only for super-Powers and, as the new
Europe becomes one of these, Britain will have to join it
if she is to make herself felt. No step, however, is more
likely to delimit the direct exercise of British influence
everywhere. If Western Europe should ever speak as a
single, unified super-Power, it will have to do so for each
of its components. Beyond "Europe," therefore, Britain
could not have a voice of her own.

Nor is that all. If Britain relinquishes overseas sources
of strength, she will not be able to do as much as antici-
pated to reshape policy within "Europe" itself.

About this, there is nothing recondite. And it is a
point that statesmen bred in the pragmatic tradition of
British public life should have been the first to detect. It
was, after all, one of them who depicted the Holy Alliance—that exalted regal forerunner of the Common
Market—as "a piece of sublime mysticism and nonsense."

Today, the process by which the Six integrates could scarcely be less high-flown or more mundane. But whatever may be practical for the Common Market may not be practical for Britain because of the adverse effect that membership would have on Britain's role. Not that mysticism is what makes Europeanizers burke such realities. It would be odd, nevertheless, if the spirit of Tsar Alexander I rather than that of Lord Castlereagh were to haunt some of their more nebulous theories.

Nobody knows what the "top table," if there is one, will be like. Occupants of its American seat, at any rate, may yet recognize that Britain can be of more use to the free world by keeping an individual capacity than by forgoing it. But that is a truth that others might overlook unless the British people themselves make it clear. And they cannot make it clear until they have set their own house in order.

XX SEMANTICS AND THE SCALE OF THINGS

In a great debate like Britain's the same terms are employed to mean different things. A century ago there were those who wished to discard overseas ties, and they were dubbed Little Englanders. Now Little Englanders, in the view of some Europeanizers, are those who stick to overseas ties and who will oppose the submergence of Britain in a European union.

By the same token, what is isolationism? Britain would not repel isolationism (as some aver), but more nearly embrace it if regional links were to supplant global ones. It is patent that Britain would not only be isolating herself from overseas associates; if European associates find

her recalcitrant on the topic of total integration, she
might also be isolated from them. Britain might want to
operate within the European fold as a check on any
larger Third Force isolationism. But she is more likely to
be swayed by such an isolationism after the means for
independent action is jettisoned.

There are those who contend that the horizons of an
inward-looking Europe will be less narrow if an outward-
looking Britain belongs to it. Yet how outward-looking
will Britain be after her own overseas contacts have
dwindled or been tossed away?

Then, too, economies of scale is another vogue term
which should be subjected to more critical scrutiny than
it has been. The Common Market provides its members
with an enlargement of their domestic market and, by
joining it, Britain would enjoy the same advantages as
her main industrial competitors enjoy in research and
development, production, and sales. Though political dis-
advantages would also accrue for her and the free world,
less has been said about these. There are signs, however,
that between Europeanization and the economies of scale
some middle road can yet be marked out. And if it can,
Britain's great debate should proceed on more solid
ground.

One or two neglected aspects of this problem have
always been clear. The utmost use of economies of scale
is not required for keeping all British products competitive abroad. There might, moreover, be a growing number of British subsidiaries which can finish or sell
semifinished British products behind the protective barriers of the Common Market. Electronic computers, on
the other hand, have often been cited as key examples
of items that must be produced in a larger economy than

Britain's if British technology is to withstand its huge American competitor, or is to escape direct American ownership and control.

But a bill that seems so plausible in theory might be more difficult to fill in practice. There would, at any rate, be no outright escape from American ownership and control through amalgamation between the computer companies of Britain and France. In the French computer industry, American capital is already predominant.

Collaboration without amalgamation has, nevertheless, remained feasible. Nor is this the only field in which that is so. Political fusion has not been a *conditio sine qua non* for joint projects into which the aerospace industries of Britain, France, and European associates have been entering under official auspices. These projects arose out of a common need. Other similar needs may arise and, despite tariff barriers, may be met in the same manner.

Economies of scale, that is to say, do not exclude co-operative ventures. The entire concept might be a more adaptable one than Europeanizers, with their fixed goals, will concede. Most Europeanizers, it is true, have approved of joint projects as paving the way for complete integration. Others frown upon co-operative ventures that might leave Britain with no ace up her sleeve when her entry into "Europe" is again negotiated at Brussels. And besides, home propaganda for complete integration will ring hollow if co-operative ventures suffice.

But in Britain's great debate there is yet another debatable proposition that Europeanizers have put forth without cavil. Everybody agrees that a wider use of advanced technology will be essential as the British economy is revamped. Europeanizers have assumed, however, that for this task Britain must have access to the full range of advanced technology. They could be wrong in that assumption. All sail and no ballast, while a recipe for speed, is also one for shipwreck.

Only super-Powers, a rank to which a united Europe might aspire, can now possess the full range of advanced technology. And rather than let Britain do without access to that full range, Europeanizers would have Britain merge her identity with "Europe." But in doing this she might play herself false. A struggle to maintain an identity of her own is what Britain's crisis is all about.

No point could be more crucial than this. But for Europeanizers to admit its cogency would be to give their case away. And that raises a further point. Europeanizers have misconceived the sort of place Britain might still have in the world. Their collateral view of the coming world order, one that is appropriately cut and dried, may be no less tendentious. For the reign of super-Powers—with "Europe" and China attaining the same rank as the United States and Russia—is what they foresee. What they fear is a global oligopoly in which elbow room for Britain will be scant.

But that, surely, is not how things work. And here light may be shed by Britain's own role at the present time. For while she is not the richest ally of the United States, she does more than the others to maintain a free-world order. And she might have a similar role, one in which her function is still disproportionate, if the global structure of power undergoes further change. There is, after all, a politics as well as an economics of scale and, though the two overlap and interact, they do not wholly coincide. Even within a global oligopoly, should there be one, others might still have leeway. That would leave Britain with a certain residual scope, and if it does, the free world will reap the benefit.

A few more reflections on this point may be pertinent. As governmental entities, super-Powers would, for some latter-day Hobbes, be Leviathans writ large. And yet, in even the most highly developed countries, bigness can be overdone.

For each of them there are administrative limits. And super-Powers would not be able to break through such limits on a world stage. The bigger they become, the more susceptible they would be to an administrative law of diminishing returns. The objectives of the expansionist Chinese may be illimitable. It is, nevertheless, to limits of power within and beyond her own imperium that Russia has been adjusting herself.

As for a united Europe, it would be a queer sort of super-Power that still depended for its security on guarantees that another super-Power, the United States, still vouchsafed. And indeed it is against Third Force pretentions on the continent of Europe that a continuing separate role for Britain must also be preserved.

The United States, even if she could, would not want to act everywhere singlehandedly on behalf of the West. She does not, as Dean Rusk has said, consider herself the gendarme of the universe.[1] Others must supplement her global endeavors. But none can do as much as Britain if, on ceasing to wander in a semantic fog, the British people find themselves again.

---

1. American intervention in Vietnam had stirred up dissent over the nature of American activities abroad. In dubbing himself "sort of a neo-isolationist," George Kennan may not have meant by that term what the late Senator Robert Taft might have meant; overextension by the United States is what Senator Fulbright inveighed against. Critics have often had cause to find fault with specific American moves abroad. But even Walter Lippmann began to query the global character of American leadership in general.

Two questions remain. What would the world be like if the United States had done less than she has done since World War II? What would it be like if she were to lose heart and retrench?

XXI BRITAIN'S STATUS AND THE CITY OF LONDON

The question of Britain's entry into the Common Market
will hang fire until Paris and London are in accord.
Meanwhile, powerful elements on both sides of the
Channel are doing all they can to bring that day closer.
And disenchantment with the Commonwealth as well as
with American leadership has been serving to keep the
way open psychologically for a renewal of efforts to get
Britain into the Common Market. But such a move would
not be justified even if ties with overseas members of the
Commonwealth counted for less than they do. Some
further points that bear on the Europeanization of Britain
should therefore be cleared up.

One of these is the contention that wealth earned in
the Common Market might enable Britain to do more
economically for Commonwealth partners, developed and
underdeveloped. But would Britain be as apt to trouble
herself about them after she was Europeanized, after she
was wrapped up in continental affairs?

Here the nature of the Commonwealth is too often
glossed over. A rise in Britain's economic strength will
not suffice for other Commonwealth partners if the
British pivot of the Commonwealth is demoted inter-
nationally, if it becomes an integrated unit in a close-
knit European union. A leveling-up to equality of status
with Britain marked the evolution of the Commonwealth.
But, if Britain's own status were reduced, on what basis
could Commonwealth partners maintain the Commonwealth bond even if they wished to do so? The Commonwealth might be damaged by disputes over Common-

wealth trade agreements. If Britain's own accustomed rank were undercut, it would be doomed.

What, then, are the omens for the Commonwealth? Is it already a lost cause, a spent force, a sham? From the outset, it was riddled with anomalies. Europeanizers, nursing their chagrin over intractable non-European elements in Britain's status, may now jeer at the Commonwealth as a "gigantic farce." While it could be that, it could also be a venture—at once moral and material, traditional and experimental—that surmounts barriers of race and clime and to which wise men cling in an imperfect world. Yet not all former British dependencies have wanted to belong and today there are some who should not be there. It would be better if, having attained independence, they dropped out.

Meanwhile, Britain must not only deal with Western Europe but look beyond it. She must also look beyond any one overseas factor such as the Commonwealth (or Anglo-American friendship) in evaluating the manifold sources of British strength.

Some of these sources of strength may not rate as high as they once did. But Britain simply cannot afford to write them off. There are those who would have her choose between the Commonwealth and Europe, between Europe and the United States. She can make no such choice. What must still govern her future is a variety of connections, European and non-European, linked subtly together in a single pattern of power.

The British economy, for example, gains from what the City of London does for the world economy in banking and investment, insurance and shipping. These lucrative activities sustained Britain's status. But if Britain had not been the hub of an oceanic system, the City of London might never have achieved so outstanding a position. And how can it keep that position when Britain is Europeanized—when, as an outer island province of a European political union, she ceases to be the hub of an oceanic system?

Not that Britain's role in world finance is without domestic critics. In industry, Westminster and Whitehall may obtain co-operation between labor and management. But all British governments are more inhibited than others in the West by the volatile nature of the business which the City of London transacts, by the degree to which its fluctuations and the state of the British economy affect each other. Even the American economy, despite the magnitude of its gold reserves, is put under strain by its wider financial role.

The British pound serves as a reserve currency for the sterling area to which most members of the Commonwealth belong. As a world-wide trading currency, it is the one that is most generally used. Yet thus, too, Britain incurs liabilities which can bet met only by keeping the pound stable—a thorny task when there are periodic runs on the pound because Britain has bought more abroad than she has sold and she has been tempted to devalue again.

Sterling could not collapse without bringing down the delicate mechanism of international trade and finance. Others have therefore rallied to its support. But that meant Britain could not adopt some of the measures she might have wanted to adopt for stimulating more economic growth. And yet there must be more economic growth if disparities between imports and exports are to be wiped out as the British economy is modernized.

A "stop-go" sequence is what this harrowing conflict has produced. Attempts to resolve it are afoot. Unless it is resolved, Britain may succumb to the lures of Euro-

peanization after all, with overseas pursuits abolished and
the devil taking the hindmost.

Things have not come to such a pass as yet. One
point, however, should be made. The City of London
earns less foreign exchange through international finance
than it does through insurance and merchanting. It does
not earn enough, by any statistical estimate, to warrant
the amount of influence it exerts on the economic policies
of the nation. But when business rests on confidence,
what one section does nourishes the others. The activities
of the City of London help, moreover, to maintain London
as a world center; they should not be audited solely in
pounds, shillings, and pence. It will be well if a clash can
be avoided between the interests of the City and the
larger trading interests of the British economy. The tail
must not wag the dog. But they need each other.

In a viable British economy the City of London may
keep its accustomed position. What it cannot keep is a
self-sustaining position apart from that of the country as
a whole.

And the cogency of this last point can be illustrated
by some ruminations on probable trends across the
Channel. The more the new Europe is unified, the more
it will have to have a financial center through which the
internal transactions of a semicontinental economy may
be funneled. The City of London would be the obvious
candidate if the British Isles were not sundered from
continental neighbors by the English Channel. Equipped
for a world function, London may not be as suited geo-
graphically for a regional one. New York became the
financial capital of North America before more distant
fields beckoned. It could not have done so unless the
island of Manhattan had been virtually part of the mainland. To be sure, Amsterdam or Paris do not offer the

same expertise or possess the same facilities as London. Qualities that have made the City of London what it has been may never be duplicated elsewhere. But those qualities did not arise in a void and, if Britain is Europeanized, the circumstances under which they did arise will be recast unalterably.

An integrated Europe, moreover, will have to have a separate currency of its own. Many in Britain would like an end put to the sterling area but, if she belonged to such a Europe, the pound sterling itself would have to be abandoned.

With France drawing upon American gold reserves, President de Gaulle could also express in the monetary sphere his many-sided attempt to take the United States down a peg or two. The international payments mechanism in which the American dollar and the pound sterling are the main elements may indeed have to be reformed. American endeavors to obtain control of key French corporations have been financed by the American payments deficit. It is quite understandable that West European countries should want to devise means by which American investment can be regulated.

Proposals for a CRU, the new composite reserve unit, may or may not be adopted. But these proposals would help out the United States, and France has no desire to do that.

The upshot might be a deeper community of interest between sterling and dollar economies. Nevertheless, all this could also detract from the importance of London and New York as financial centers.

The City of London and Wall Street have been passionately "European"—in general and as far as Britain is concerned. But they are not the only ones that might find their chickens coming home to roost. So in this respect may Paris itself. The Bonn Republic is the richest segment of the Common Market and Hamburg or Frankfurt might eventually supplant others as a European financial center.

The City of London has done, and may still do, all it can to promote British entry into the Common Market. Additional business from across the Channel is what it has been expecting. And in the short run it could be right. Yet on larger issues the City of London has been far from infallible, as it own misjudgments during the appeasement era demonstrated. An oceanic complex has been the multifarious foundation of British power everywhere for a number of years. In the long run Europeanization cannot transform the status of Britain without her financial role also being curtailed.

XXII EUROPEANIZATION AND THE BRITISH POLITICAL SYSTEM

How would Europeanization affect the British political system? Over this question, too, Britain's great debate has been soft-pedaled. It is realized there can be no integration without Parliament ceding some of its sovereign powers to another, higher, more sovereign European authority. But would the functions of the Crown be the same? In one way they would not. If there were no desire to keep the Commonwealth together, Queen Elizabeth II would not be recognized as the Head of the Commonwealth by Commonwealth Republics as well as by Commonwealth Monarchies. With the Commonwealth itself signifying less and less, there would be a commensurate atrophy in the Commonwealth function of the Crown.

It is not inconceivable, on the other hand, that room

could be found in a federalized Europe for local monarchies—for those of Britain, the Low Countries, and
Scandinavia. Lesser kingdoms and various grand duchies,
after all, did grace the constitutional setup of the Imperial
German autocracy until 1918. Not that this should be
deemed a flattering precedent for a country with Britain's outstanding political tradition—one that could still
have an important role of its own. The merits of parliamentary government in Britain greatly surpass its demerits. By helping to make this work, the British Mon-
archy is not an obsolete relic but part of a living organism.
And that being so, everything depends on the vigor of
the organism as a whole.

Its vigor, moreover, is not merely a matter of concern
to the British people or to the peoples of Commonwealth
democracies overseas. To cramp the style of the British
political system would be to dim the cause of freedom
everywhere. There can be no representative democracy
in Communist lands, while in most of Asia and Africa
it does not as yet stand much of a chance. Nobody knows
what its future will be in France, West Germany, and
Italy. If things could be done as well under the American
form of representative democracy as under the British,
the United States would have led the West with more
dexterity. The political system that (despite all its defects) can still set standards is rare. In its perpetuation,
others have a stake.

But what about the adaptability of the British Constitution? Would not this virtue, one for which it has
been famed, prove useful? If Britain is Europeanized, the
adaptability of her political system might prove of little
use in any situation that could arise. A century has passed
since Canada started the vogue for incorporating the
essentials of the unwritten, unitary British Constitution

within a written federal constitution. What could now result, however, is not a synthesis between two different methods, but the actual subordination of one to another— the prospect of having the historic unwritten British Constitution yield to an over-all written European constitution in the more decisive spheres of governance.

Economic integration alone would not bring that about. An accompanying change in Britain's own political milieu would make it more difficult for her to retard institutional change. The British Constitution has shown itself flexible and able to keep up with the times. There was full play for these attributes—both at home and overseas—within a political bailiwick where Britain's own writ ran, or within a Britannic realm where a resilient British tradition predominated. Britain's own writ will not run, a resilient British tradition will not predominate, across the English Channel. It would be hard enough for an integrated Britain to get her own way in the field of diplomacy. Constitutionally, in the major spheres of governance, an integrated Britain would have still less chance of holding on.

XXIII NATO AND NEUTRALISM

The Europeanization of Britain would be a leap in the dark both politically and economically. This step has been urged, nevertheless, as a means of reducing risks in other domains. Close integration with European neighbors, it has been suggested, would help Britain to prevent a recurrence of 1914 and 1939. But those who say this should recall how international affairs have altered and what is being done about them. In 1914 and 1939 the issue of peace or war turned on a European balance of power without an American contribution. Today Western Europe is but one sector of a global balance that the United States does most to maintain.

NATO and the American nuclear deterrent did not exist in 1914 and 1939. Nor is there anything in NATO that obliges Britain to accept commitments exceeding those undertaken by the United States, Canada, or European allies beyond the gates of the Common Market.

But what if the British people balk at Europeanization? Would that be a sign of neutralism? Neutralism can express itself in a number of ways. There is one version that Afro-Asian countries expound. There is a classic European brand which neutrals such as Switzerland, Sweden, and Austria observe. And now there are some in Britain who, with their policy of free rides, purvey a brand of their own.

In the Orient, where neutralism is often inescapable, neutralists are not always anti-American. But there is always an anti-American streak in the political escapism of Western neutralists. What they, too, frequently overlook is how peacekeeping by the United States outweighs American errors. To those errors a united Europe has been envisaged as a corrective. If Britain were caught up in a Third Force, she would go neutralist through Europeanization and not by abstaining from it.[1]

It is, in other words, not between co-operation and nonco-operation that Britain must decide, but between types of co-operation that are diverse and could be antagonistic.

Britain cannot lay undue stress on Europe without

1. Political escapism in British life appears to cut across differences of class and doctrine. It could be seen among proponents of British entry into the Common Market (see section X above) to whom the appeasement of Russia and China would be repugnant. It impels those among neutralists and nuclear disarmers who may have been against British entry into the Common Market but who, like the prewar appeasers of Hitler and Mussolini, would now appease Russia or China.

the Commonwealth dissolving, without there being dislocations in the Orient as well as in the Occident by which the free world might be set back. Where, too, would Britain be if close co-operation with Europe derogated from Atlantic co-operation and the defense of the West were thus impaired? The British people should accept modifications of autonomy by which all the principal members of the North Atlantic Alliance might be bound together more closely. But they must beware of a tight integration within restricted European confines that could split NATO and paralyze the West.

A Paris-Bonn axis might have had a Third Force as its outcome. Britain would throw her weight against such an array and that was why, in the eyes of General de Gaulle, the new Europe could do best without her— though she might be more compliant and, therefore, less unclubbable after her Commonwealth and Anglo-American bonds had been discarded.

British sources of strength were thus analyzed with a shrewdness lacking in many of the French President's critics. And yet the French themselves, since 1914, have indirectly owed much to these overseas sources of British strength. That is what President de Gaulle misconceived. But the French have no monopoly on misconceptions.

To debar serious rifts between the United States and a united Europe or heal them when they occur—that is a task for which Britain is peculiarly suited. It would, however, be a task requiring more of a free hand than Europeanization would leave her and one necessitating a more solid backing among some European elements than she can invariably rely on. The United States, as a transatlantic guarantor of European security, might soon rue the day that an individual British capacity in European and world politics was not preserved. But so, above all, might Britain herself.

How Good Are the British?

XXIV MARGIN FOR ERROR

Ever since World War I and the misjudgments that cul-
minated in World War II, there have been no soft
options for the British people. Two centuries ago, when
the American colonies were about to revolt, Adam Smith
wrote that Britain should accommodate herself to "the
real mediocrity of her circumstances." Britain did not have
to take this advice because during the years that lay
ahead there was nothing mediocre in her circumstances
or, with all her faults, in the service she rendered. But
mediocrity within is what could now make her circumstances still more mediocre. And this is what must first be
combated.

How good are the British? Their status in the world
depends on the reply tendered this basic question.
Though the Industrial Revolution started in Britain, she
was less advanced than the United States or Imperial
Germany in technology even before the dawn of the
twentieth century. But other gifts served. And it was by
abjuring these that Britain did most, after World War I,
to set herself back. Political intangibles such as ties with
Commonwealth countries and Anglo-American friendship,
fortunately, could still be called into play. Today these
political intangibles will not be worth much unless there

is a change of heart among the British people, unless intangibles that will revivify and modernize are also brought into play.

No other major people has had to operate within so small a margin for error. And it was from failure to grasp this cardinal truth that Britain in the 1930's failed herself. More recently those among the British who craved entry into the Common Market fancied that domestic maladies might be cured by severing overseas ties. But the prescription was one for which Britain would have had to write a blank check politically—while, in economic terms, the price might also have been exorbitant. Foreign trade is Britain's lifeblood, and it is not by bloodletting of the body politic that this lifeblood can be enriched.

It would be painful for any great people to reconcile themselves with grace to so abrupt a come-down in world rank. What the British must not do is reconcile themselves to the second best on the home front. Primacy in the West has shifted across the Atlantic to the United States, while in the East the Soviet Union still has the lead. Proponents of a European Third Force expect it to rank as a first-rate Power. But if Britain exercises first-rate powers she might still be in a category of her own.

Nor is there any mystery about this. Where economic or political strength derives from land mass or territorial coherence, what is relinquished in one generation can sometimes be retrieved in another. It does not evaporate. This is how the French and West German Republics—quite apart from titans such as the United States, Russia, and China—have been able to get away with much that would have ruined Britain irremediably long ago. When power reposes on the solid, visible foundations of an area that is compact and richly endowed, it looms up as a natural phenomenon, while an inheritance that is

widely scattered and wholly man-made seems more arti-
ficial. Britain became the hub of an oceanic complex
through accident rather than design. In maintaining her
world status there was more design than accident.

It was skill, after all, that enabled Britain to underwrite a free-world order—one in which other countries
flourished, and one which the kindred people of the
United States, on replacing her, did most to preserve.

The British, however, began to lose their touch when
they assumed pre-eminence had been foreordained. And
they must uproot remnants of that fallacy before they
again make their way.

Imponderables such as intelligence, proficiency, and
integrity were elements of power whose utility could not
be fathomed until they ran short after World War I—
until misjudgment, self-willed and self-defeating, was ele-
vated by popular consent into a principle of British statecraft. Britain, with Churchill to inspire her, averted defeat. She did this by her own exertions and through the
support of those across the seas whose stake in British
resistance was so great. A middle stance between primacy
and decline should now be her aim. Means for sustaining
it still elude her.

XXV INCENTIVES AND CLASS DIVISIONS

Britain will lack the means for sustaining a middle stance
between primacy and decline until the latent gifts of the
British people can be again evoked and deftly put to
use. The objective of all parties is a higher rate of economic growth without inflation. But now, with economic
growth halted as debt repayments are made, unemployment is what may grow. The fact remains, as the indices

rise and fall, that the energies of the British people cannot be released on an adequate scale until there are more incentives for getting ahead.

Britain labors under the same economic handicaps as other industrialized countries of the West—unrest among workers over the advent of automation, job monotony, communist intrigue, wildcat strikes, managerial obtuseness, new forms of organizational and corporate privilege.

Yet here, too, Britain is a special case. While classes may be less stratified than they once were, habits of mind that have a class origin still accentuate socio-economic differences. Even under communism, it is by rewarding the ambitious that things are kept going.

The Welfare State has not made the masses content with their lot. Yet few seek to improve their lot by personal achievement. There is sloth instead. This may be a kind of protest vote against social inequities. But it is by regalvanizing and not by passively dragging down the British economy that these social inequities can finally be mitigated. It would seem as though the masses, glum, lethargic and self-immured, do not wish to break the very class bounds that restrain them and that they resent.

One upshot is the air of irrelevance in which the conventional rivalry of Left and Right is steeped. Class divides North Americans less than race or color. But the British are still so divided by class that, in a progressive economy, class divisions tend merely to be reduplicated on a higher economic plane. Britain's social inequities are not as tragic as those to which American Negroes are subject—though she, too, has a color problem with immigration from nonwhite countries of the Commonwealth. There also is no parallel to the rift between the French-speaking and English-speaking communities of Canada—a rift which dampens Canada's recent promise as a Middle Power. All the same, there is less in the class structure of North America that is economically self-inhibiting, less of a tendency for one to accept meekly the station to which one is born.

European critics may allege that a crass materialism, with its prize of higher living standards, is what has actuated Americans and Canadians. But where the economy vegetates, there is a falling away in every branch of endeavor, material and nonmaterial.

What will determine Britain's future is Britain's own capacity to take herself in hand. It may be that if there had been less party strife during the bright delusive twilight of the late Victorian and post-Victorian eras, Britain might not have rested on her economic oars. Western civilization never recovered from World War I, and Britain, as its main buttress, will never be the same again. After the flower of British youth was struck down, men of lesser talent took over. Antics that brought on World War II stemmed traumatically from World War I.

As with World War I, the after-effects of World War II were also delayed. The Welfare State was not all that cushioned the shock; so did American loans, Marshall aid, financial assistance from Canada, and the false prosperity of the 1950's. Then there was always that legendary British stiff upper lip to rely on. But this, too, is not what it used to be. Britain was put on her mettle in 1940 by enemy action. Now she must cope with slow attrition from within.

What renders Britain's predicament so acute is not only her narrower margin for error, but the fact that the morale of the country has sagged. Before people will bestir themselves, they must have something to which they can look forward. Britain is not as classbound as she was when, according to Disraeli, she consisted of two nations; the mobility of classes could now be as great as in other English-speaking democracies. But it would be a mobility with a difference—and within limits. Nowhere else in the West are social groups so graded by accent and schooling. Not that everything is stratified. The number of those who do not fit into a polarized social register has been increasing. And yet only in Britain could even the classless be regarded as a class.

Nor is that all. The lower and middle segments, even when disgruntled, tend to admire and thus protract the social ideology of the upper crust. Elsewhere in the West a fresh economic impetus may come from the top. Britain's ruling ideology militates against one.

A patrician ethos still sets the pattern of success among the British people. And this is perpetuated by plutocrats who have bought their way socially into the leisure class—or into what has remained of it.

Business itself, however, has set the pattern of success in North America—though it, too, has had its own cult of privilege. Nothing did more ideologically to put steam into American capitalism than the popular belief that all have the same chance; that what pioneers and immigrants once did, others can still do. From rags to riches, from log cabin to the White House—the inequalities of latter-day American life have taken the shine out of these venerated clichés. But although there is much in the American economy that is morally equivocal, it has an inner vitality that keeps it alert, if only by fits and starts. On both sides of the Atlantic, where there is bigness, spontaneity may be deadened, individuality stifled, and dissent foreclosed. And yet, though American capitalism is not what it was, pre-corporate incentives do still lend vigor to the American economy. But in the home of the Industrial Revolution, British equivalents are now less at home.

At this turning point, all the same, pre-corporate incentives are what Britain needs most. When she was pre-eminent, the leisure class had a rich country to govern, an empire to administer, a lead to take on every sector of world affairs. However, apart from these activities, and from sport, the rulers of Britain seldom had their heart in other essential pursuits—and leisure-class values seeped down. This seepage would be welcome if it comprised ideals of duty and *noblesse oblige,* but among leisure-class values, the more self-indulgent ones are what now pervade other British classes.[1]

It may be a first step toward better things when we do what we are doing as well as we can. Britain today is full of people who feel they were cut out for better things, but will scarcely lift a finger to achieve them.

This is no laughing matter. When the leisure class flourished, it laid stress on consumption rather than production because surpluses were created by others. These surpluses were often created by entrepreneurs who, looking up to the leisure class and having joined it, would kick away the very ladder on which they had made their ascent. But, in a more straitened mass economy, there cannot be the same stress on consumption without everything being put out of joint.

Would lassitude disappear if the British economy as a whole were socialized? That would not dispose of leisure-class values to which the leisure class itself has clung too long and which other classes have been premature in adopting. The Welfare State was a necessity, one which could not have been postponed. But some of the leisure-

1. Fox hunting has had a leisure-class cachet, and that may be why some coal miners in South Wales have taken it up. In no other country would such a sport attract them. An amusing piece of news, it is also a good sign that they can afford to do this after years of deprivation. That they should want to do it may not be a good sign at all.

class values that have been superimposed upon the Welfare State are a luxury—and they would clog national energies under any economic system that Britain might have today.

Nor would class differences be utterly dispelled by a social revolution. Class differences, after all, emerge in more egalitarian societies—in a free one like that of the United States, and in an unfree one like that of the Soviet Union. While class differences may yet subside in Britain, she dare not wait for them to shrivel up entirely. The primordial question for her is whether, in spite of class differences, the British people can be persuaded to try harder.

It is the unique position which Britain holds that makes the crisis by which she is dogged so bewildering. This, however, is something the British people themselves do not always remember. The war evoked a singleness of purpose that peacetime, by its sheer multiplicity of problems, cannot evoke. Then, too, there is all the buck-passing, that concomitant of bigness, which slows things up when they should be accelerated.

Signs of progress of a sort, nevertheless, are visible in many spheres. New buildings, for instance, have been altering British skylines. The Victorians did much to make Britain ugly. It is regrettable that these needed new buildings do not improve matters. Nowadays it is some of Britain's beautiful, smaller historic cities that are having their hearts torn out. As for London, it had wounds to lick after the Nazi blitz and a building boom to oversee. The British metropolis could have been redeveloped by the sort of plan through which Paris has preserved most, though not all, of its famous contours. There is no such plan. London might have borrowed from the best of recent North American architecture for postwar reconstruction. While the imitations are numerous, most are poor.

Here, as elsewhere, are the stigmata of a mass economy and of the large-scale technology by which it is sustained. Yet here, too, is proof, drab though it may be, that Britain is not being left behind.

There has been progress, too, in the redistribution of wealth between various segments of the populace, but that will have been in vain if it only makes Britain live beyond her means. Self-renewal should be the aim. Without it self-immobilization may ensue.

The British people can scarcely thrive by taking in each other's washing. Nevertheless, there appears to have been more of this than the economy can afford. An excess of imports over exports may set the alarm bells ringing; a change of outlook all down the line has yet to come. The result, moreover, is that while the British still expect others to have confidence in them they are losing confidence in themselves. The grave sterling crisis of 1964-66 was provoked by the huge deficit in the British balance of payments and by the way it was being handled. Foreign speculators were not the only ones who sold the pound short and caused flights from sterling.[2]

The central banks of other countries saved the day. By so doing they prevented a breakdown in the international payments system and thus in international trade. They also prevented a wider political breakdown—that further abridgment of the British role by which the well-being of the entire free world would be affected so adversely. For Britain has to help maintain the balance of power—and her books must be balanced if she is to meet commitments without difficulty.

2. Friends and allies took umbrage before this when, contrary to international agreements, import surcharges were imposed and exports subsidies promulgated.

It is, of course, only by a rise in exports that Britain can pay her way and that is the goal toward which her plans for economic growth must be directed. An incomes policy, if one ever does take shape, may quicken these plans. If employees, employers, and investors accept its restraints, they will have joined hands at last. Yet whatever checks inflation and reduces the number of strikes may also check growth. It was to resolve contradictions such as these that the National Plan, as published in 1965, was laid down. The Government itself must also spend less. Natural gas finds on land and in the North Sea gasfields may, however, prove a good omen. If they decrease some British fuel imports, there may be less of a deficit in the balance of payments. But, as all will stagnate without greater productivity, massive new investment may be required. And this might be hard to procure until there is evidence that it will be put to the best possible use.

In the end, the problem is one of morale—the assiduity of the British people, the extent to which they apply themselves to the economic renovation of their country.

The circumstances of the war and postwar reconstruction may explain why, as compared with the industry of trade rivals, there is so much that is obsolescent on both sides of British industry. But more than business will suffer if all classes, with reflexes conditioned to one epoch, do not have those reflexes reconditioned to another.

XXVI SOURCES OF PRESTIGE

Britain must find new economic stimuli. But these are not all that may bolster the British role. There also are features of British life that have been identified with the leisure class in a positive rather than negative sense.

Whatever renders British life distinctive, still enhances British prestige. Leisure-class values cannot be eradicated. The right tactic should be to circumvent in the British social system what is morally or economically wrong and to exploit what can be justifiably exploited.

In the political sphere, during the campaign for British entry into the Common Market, there were those on the Right and at the Center who were prepared quite untraditionally to cast away traditional British sources of overseas strength. So, too, there are cultural sources of domestic strength with which the Left, when it insists on a drastic overhaul of British society, could be as improvident. For what is lacking in these various programs, whether of the Right, Left, or Center, is a consideration from which all who grapple with the British problem should start. This is that no oversimplified solution will suffice because the multi-faceted British role, in which so much was made out of so little, can never be a simple one.

It is, for instance, as agencies of leisure-class values that British public schools have been under fire. These are, in fact, the most private of institutions and it is as private schools that their American (and Canadian) counterparts are known. In the United States, however, it is less usual even for the affluent to have their sons (or daughters) educated at an early stage away from home. American public schools are genuinely public and, in racially desegregated areas of the country, they have made an immense contribution to American nationhood by assimilating so many of diverse antecedents. Class segregation, on the other hand, is what British public schools have been accused of promoting. And it is proper that they should take in a larger percentage of boys from working-class families if funds can be furnished.

Better than the average public school, moreover, are a number of grammar and State secondary schools. But for Britain to abolish public schools entirely might be to do more harm than good. On the debit side they have fostered class divisions; on the credit side the best have provided the intellectual substratum for those elite standards that Oxford and Cambridge have upheld, but which extended far beyond them. Prestige and power are not unrelated and the contribution that elite standards can still make to British prestige should never be minimized.

A point which those who would scrap British public schools tend to overlook may be reiterated here. This is that more than the mechanism of British society has been at fault. There can therefore be no certitude that structural changes will induce changes in other essential spheres; few, after all, followed from the social reforms of the Welfare State. Morally and politically these social reforms could not have been withheld. They have not, however, made a larger number of British workers more productive or more efficient. By the same token, to abolish public schools entirely may be merely to equalize on a lower rather than on a higher plane. The danger is great, too, that talent will be congealed at a tender age by the curricula of State schools, and even by colleges or universities when they crowd out young people whose abilities ripen late. If Britain is still to play an important part, it is a leveling-up rather than a leveling-down that must be the goal. This is a goal, moreover, toward which less classbound democracies must also strive from another angle.

Britain has energies that have been blocked and must be released. Class privilege is not the only sort of privilege that blocks a fuller release of these energies. Fewer British scientists, for example, might emigrate to the

United States if institutional hierarchies did not hobble scientific research in Britain. And then there is the unusual handicap under which the engineering profession labors. For it ranks less high, in the eyes of employers and the general public, than it does across the Atlantic. Eingineering therefore does not attract as many as it should among those who qualify for technical training—though Britain, in the age of technology, will require all the engineers she can get.

Here are forms of caste with which other social divisions have little to do, and reordering the British economy may not eliminate them. There are, besides, inverted snobberies—the way in which the uninitiated suspect those of their own kind who have acquired learning. And this intramural prejudice will not necessarily dissolve when more working-class boys are admitted to public schools, or when general facilities for advanced training have been multiplied. There is not the same estrangement from families and native surroundings among students of humble origin in the United States, Canada, Australia, and New Zealand.

A cleavage between classes is not all by which Britain is beset. There are cleavages that cut across classes; there is even an alienation from society as a whole. Those alienated from American society are proportionately less numerous—though sizable minorities (race and color being more immutable than class) have deeper grievances. A release of energies on the American model is what Britain must elicit.

At its best, education in Britain has had a quality that Americans could profitably seek to cultivate, but schooling for an elite is an extravagance if not adapted to what must be an altered role for Britain on the world scene. In Britain the task is to enlarge the scale of things without lowering standards. And if that can be accomplished, British society may transform itself from within.

As for the American mass democracy, it has seldom taken elite standards as its guide. But now, with Russia advancing in science and technology and with Western Europe resurgent, elite standards are what the United States as leader of the West must do her utmost to maintain. One third of young Americans, as contrasted with eight per cent among the British, get a chance to attend a college or university of one sort or another, yet such figures would be more reassuring if American education were not spread so thin.

In some branches of endeavor, Britain may merely antagonize friends and partners by hugging illusions of superiority when superiority has dwindled. In others, it is precisely through a well-founded superiority that she can still make herself felt. This is the heart of Britain's dilemma.

In industry the products on which the British will have to concentrate are the ones that do not call for massive facilities such as the semicontinental areas of the United States, the Soviet Union, or even a united Europe might command. Other economies flourish without having to manufacture all types of long-range aircraft and electronic computers.

Targets for tomorrow will have to be selected with the same empiric acumen as made the British people, in both politics and business, what they once were. These targets can be hit only if the British economy again vibrates with zest and expertise. But it cannot do so until all classes realize what has distinguished their country from others: the fact that, in Britain, intangibles have affected tangibles more than elsewhere because the resourcefulness of

her own people has been her most precious national re-
source. And this will not endure of its own accord, by a
mere stroke of luck. It has to be worked at.

Britain's chief hope lies in spheres where superiority
can still be vindicated. One of these spheres, is that of the
English language—the competence with which the British people, in comparison with other English-speaking
peoples, use the Queen's English. In Britain, as in no other
English-speaking country, leisure-class accents have, like
public schools, erected a barrier between classes. Yet
language barriers may not be insuperable. Radio and
popular education have been rendering enunciation and
intonation more uniform—though this, in turn, might
impair local dialects. Welsh is a separate language, but a
dialect like that of the Scots is to the British what the
accent of the American South is to the North and West
of the United States. As for the argot of the British work-
ing class, seldom is it dull.

The point to be noticed in this connection is how, in
everyday English usage, even the semieducated in Britain
often express themselves with more felicity than literate
Americans, Canadians, or Australians. English speech
could not be transplanted to the soil of North America
without being altered by pioneer life, and new transatlantic versions were what later European immigrants
learned. There was always an elite to uphold standards
of speech in Britain; none lasted long enough overseas
to do this. English as spoken in North America is lively
in idiom, but flat in tone. If its range were broader, fewer
crudities would creep in and, in the presence of British
intellectual inferiors, educated Americans would not, as
they often are, be so ill at ease linguistically. Yet against
all this must be set the supreme fact that the United
States speaks English—a fact with a significance that

impressed itself upon Bismarck in the nineteenth century and a major factor in the shaping of events in the twentieth ·century.

Britain still has an empire, a cultural one, on which the sun never sets. At a time when she must adapt herself to diminished power, she has, in the English language, an impalpable counter that still carries undiminished weight. British actors do well on both sides of the Atlantic; they are to the fore when television and motion pictures carry the English tongue to more distant lands. Radio, however, must do more than entertain. For that is a sphere in which the external services of the British Broadcasting Corporation have, like the Voice of America, been withstanding Russian, Chinese, and Egyptian attempts to subvert neutral countries. Britain today does not have a message for the air waves as compelling as that conveyed to others when she was the spearhead of the struggle against Hitler. But in the domain of language and literature she still walks among the lords of the earth. The existence of that domain serves the cause of the West. And Britain cannot be shoved into a corner as long as it does exist.

The cultural tie between Britain and the United States is a familiar theme. But the use of the English language by former British dependencies has, despite the anticolonial upsurge, also strengthened the hand of the West against the East in those countries.

Among developing countries, the struggle for influence is fought on a number of planes; even when it goes against the West on one plane, there is another plane on which both Peking and Moscow are habitually outmatched. Many developing countries use the English language for overcoming a babel of tongues at home, and for communicating with English-speaking mentors across the seas. Such use may infuriate xenophobes, but it is the only way in which the national unity of some key developing countries can ever be forged.

Culture has long been an instrument of policy for the French. But this is the one realm in which there are no serious disparities between the United States and Britain. The United States, on the contrary, has found an unanticipated utility in the cultural overlap of the English-speaking peoples; nothing did more to expedite her own new world-wide contacts when she took Britain's place as leader of the West. Increments of prestige in the Anglo-American cultural field must, to some extent, always be shared. And, so far as Britain is concerned, they will be neither unearned nor undeserved.[1]

1. The fact is, nevertheless, that Britain and the United States still treat such pursuits in a haphazard fashion and that it was left for France, as custodian of the creative spirit, to establish a Ministry of Culture. In 1964 the British people were given a junior minister to look after leisure and the arts. First assigned with sheepish if typical incongruity to the Ministry of Public Building and Works, she was later moved to the Department of Education and Science.

For cultural activities abroad, however, Britain has the British Council, while the United States has her Fulbright Scholarships and her Information Agency—not all the libraries which the latter provides being in cities where they may be stoned or burned down. There was an outcry in India against a proposal to endow an Indian-American foundation with rupees owned by the United States. Then, too, an Assistant Secretary of State for Educational and Cultural Affairs has been added to the American State Department. A relatively picayune sum was, besides, granted by Congress in 1965 for setting up a governmental foundation for the arts and humanities. Within the Department of Health, Education and Welfare there is also a Center for Educational Co-operation. The sciences, of course, have been endowed with a lavish hand. But a Ministry of Culture, even a junior minister, is still far to seek.

Between *Kultur*, as promoted before 1914 by the goose-stepping German Empire, and the invincible Philistinism of Anglo-American public life, the French have been occupying some middle ground.

Paris, for example, has long been a lodestar for the intellectuals of Latin America as well as for the rich and fashionable. Latin-American concepts of democracy are in the French tradition. More direct is the politico-cultural influence that France still exerts among former African colonies, while in Indo-China, too, much of that influence remains. Within the West itself, the French-speaking sections of Belgium

Then there is travel—a related field and one in which manners can be a prestige element. Not all the British who exhibit upper-class manners when they go abroad belong to the upper class; but in countries accustomed to class deference these manners earn a grudging respect. And here the average American tourist may not do as well. British *savoir-faire* can often be accompanied by a certain upperclass standoffishness. This, nevertheless, may not offend others as much as either the bonhomie or spleen of the more classless Americans.

Worldly and well-bred Americans know what is done and what is not done across the Atlantic. But they may be outnumbered by the purse-proud on the one hand, and by the thrifty on the other; by those who, like *nouveaux riches* everywhere, have yet to learn that there are some things money cannot buy; and by those who, with few pennies to spare, will not let avaricious European hosts overcharge them. Recently, however, British types to which continentals are less accustomed have been taking their holidays on the European continent.

The manners of these British trippers, like those of football fans or commercial travelers up in London from the provinces on a spree, are neither more nor less callow than those of American tourists in the mass. Upon Europeans the impression they leave may be much the same.

---

and Switzerland are, of course, next door. Elsewhere there is (in contrast to more numerous English-speaking areas) only Quebec.

Separatist tendencies have been dividing French-speaking Canadians from their English-speaking compatriots. Anything France does to encourage these tendencies could impair the unity of Canada and thus be against the interests of the West.

Quebec, in true Gallic style, has its own Ministry of Culture and this innovation would be entirely to the credit of that Province if it had no ulterior political motive. Like Britain and the United States, Canada, as a whole, does not have a Ministry of Culture. But, for encouragement of the arts and scholarship, there is the Canada Council.

And yet among the English-speaking people themselves Britain has a self-sustaining prestige advantage in the domain of travel. Many strands of the American, Canadian, and Antipodean past come from the British Isles; these have been converted into hard cash. American tourists bring in more dollars than any single British export industry.

Then, too, "swinging London," with its sham gaiety, may have given a further spurt to the number of visitors from the United States as well as from Western Europe. Some of this might have been due to a less entertaining atmosphere in that other tourist Mecca, the waspish, puffed-up and high-priced Paris of de Gaulle. Among the young in Britain, phenomena as hectic as the cult of the Beatles, pop music and avant-garde clothes may have arisen from the spirit of eat, drink and be merry for tomorrow we die. Now, when Britain is undergoing a new, mild bout of economic austerity, all must buckle down to work. But as "swinging London" earned foreign exchange and promoted the sale of British consumer goods abroad, it did offer an amusing counterpoint to that economic self-throttling by which Britain is so grievously afflicted.

By way of contrast, travel in North America rather than across the English Channel has been limited for most British tourists by its greater cost and by British restrictions on the amount of dollars they may purchase. Americans and Canadians have not therefore been seen as much in their home environment—something which, as the Common Market campaign revealed, could have long-term consequences.

But those hardy perennials, visiting British lecturers, still get paying American audiences—and a few, on their return home, may still write articles about their American hosts that are as condescending or as derisive as any penned by Victorian, Edwardian, or Georgian predecessors. This has always been a one-way traffic. Aemricans (and Canadians) are as curious as ever about British views, and some of the British are as eager as ever to satisfy them. About American views, or the views of others, the bulk of the British people have been and remain less curious.

XXVII OTHER ADVANTAGES

While language, literature, travel, the attractions of the historic and picturesque may be turned to account, Britain has still other prestige advantages that should also be considered.

One of these is in the realm of wearing apparel, and it has a social significance that is less trivial than it seems. Subnationalities like the Scots and the Welsh and many of the emergent nationalisms of Asia and Africa can assert themselves in national dress. The British do not need to do anything of the sort as others are deemed incorrect when they do not ape the British. Formal dress, as the vestigial trapping of leisure-class rituals, is still worn more often in Britain than in the United States. But the old school tie is peculiar to Britain, a class symbol which is potent without being worn. So, too, it is from leisure-class preoccupation with dress that criteria of what the well-dressed man will wear are derived and passed down. Only a few can have attended the right schools or served with the right regiments. Others, suitably garbed, may bear themselves as though they had.

In a less expansive period than that of Elizabeth I, Beau Brummel or even the Edwardian dandy, it is the female of the species who might do most to attract attention. The mini-skirted girls of Chelsea reflect a new *mores*. But some young men of the lower middle class could only adorn themselves in the foppish raiment of Carnaby Street when jobs were overabundant. With the return of hard times, they may not be as able to afford such finery. Among their elders and betters, however, many are still meticulously conservative in their dress.

"Manners makyth man," said William of Wykeham, but nowhere more than in London, with its own inimitable stamp, is style also the man. All free peoples have their own mixtures of individuality and conformity. Yet there is one London submixture which is not that of the mass age and which, in its outer guise, seems oblivious to change in Britain's world position.[1]

Wherever there has been a leisure class, or wherever there are any who aspire to join it, men as well as women have an eye for the niceties of dress. Socially the Court of St. James's tops everything. For London's sartorial ambiance, nevertheless, much is still owed to hatters like James Lock of St. James's Street; to bespoke tailors in

1. The British, like other Western peoples, also have those who, with long uncut hair or shapeless unkempt beards, cultivate a slovenly appearance. Soldiers have to be neat; but today in Britain, where the military tradition is at a discount, the military crop is no longer prescribed for the British Army. By way of contrast the American crew-cut, with its somewhat Germanic hint of military discipline and martial severities, became more widespread across the Atlantic after World War II—at a time when the United States was so largely saddled with the defense of the free world.

Mods and Rockers have also found comfort in nonconformist conformity. In their holiday clashes at British seaside resorts each teen-age gang has had a distinctive group costume as its own uniform battle regalia.

So, too, when the Campaign for Nuclear Disarmament held its Easter marches, nonconformist conformity could express itself through more than slogans and speeches, cheers and chants. Beatnik vesture and disheveled plumage—the *dernier cri* for most participants of both sexes—also had become political emblems.

the vicinity of Savile Row; to outfitters in the environs
of Jermyn Street and Bond Street; to the umbrella makers
of Piccadilly. And among these arbiters of fashion, the
hatters are the ones who do most to maintain British
prestige.

Nor is it only against the threat of the hatless or the
revolt of beatniks and Beatles that they nostalgically hold
the fort. They have the dignity of the bowler hat to defend against the nondescript English trilby or American
snap-brim fedora and even against that more solemn
black Homburg that was identified, because of Anthony
Eden, with the Foreign Office in prewar days. A piece of
London headgear that belongs nowhere else, the bowler
does most to give London clubmen, as distinguished from
less modish contemporary types, an air of elegance, authority, and self-assurance so reminiscent of vanished
British splendors.

Dark suits with an impeccable cut, white starched
collars of an approved shape, tightly folded umbrellas—
these provide a frame for the picture. A bowler hat—
smart in contour and with a rakish tilt—is what crowns
it all. As class insignia these are details of a masculine
ensemble that only the more rash in the business circles
of the City and West End, or only the more egalitarian
among those at Westminster and Whitehall who govern
the country, would dare to impugn. A bank clerk in
London may have less chance than a bank clerk in New
York of becoming a bank director. But when properly
clad, he is more apt than a Wall Street tycoon to resemble one.

London, with its stately institutional façade, can avoid
the fate of Imperial Vienna or divided Berlin. As a world
center there is still plenty for it to do. But only in London

do so many have the simple knack, through trim, fastidi-
ous, characteristic attire, of making themselves seem more
important than they are.

In maintaining British prestige, as a matter of fact,
London has always had a dominant role. One secret of
British primacy was the means the British possessed of
extending British influence beyond the limits of British
power—and London's civic stature could be numbered
among them. It still can. While the limits of British power
have shrunk, London's capacity to extend British influence beyond the limits of British power has not shrunk
as much. For what London does is bring the multiple
activities of a great nation to a single focus—something
that Paris or Rome can also do, but something for which
Washington, Ottawa, or Canberra is unequipped.

And the advantage that Britain thus still enjoys may
be measured by the disadvantage under which the United
States labors in the absence of any one comparable
American focal point. The American Government has its
seat in Washington; New York, however, is the American
capital for business and thought, taste and culture. London offers at a single center mutually stimulating contacts
between those in charge of every national pursuit. Washington cannot do that. American governance is one of
divided powers between nation and states; between the
President, the Congress and the Supreme Court. These
divided powers are what differentiate the American political system from the British political system with its
unitary powers. Washington symbolizes a division of
powers that is more than constitutional.

The capital city of the United States is no longer the
raw, bleak, cultural wilderness by which Henry Adams
and American notables of his period were once so dis-
tressed. But it would not be as difficult for New York to

supplant Washington as it would be for Washington to supplant New York. Around London, on the other hand, British industry and commerce are now more concentrated than they were during the nineteenth century. An over-concentration that drains the provinces may be as bad for Britain as it is for France. But London would have less utility as an instrument of British prestige if so many branches of national activity did not intermix so constantly within it. All Washington can do is create the political image of the United States—one that does not always do justice to the underlying virtues of the American people. In every walk of life, London does most to create the British image.

Will it be a true or false one? A deterioration in the quality of British endeavors must eventually be found out. But even where the British are no better than others, they can proceed as though they are.

Much that is first rate in the intellectual and creative life of North America may be frustrated when it is removed from the center. In Britain, however, nobody is ever very far from the center and merely being there enables the second-rate to project itself beyond its merits. Nor is the sounding board to which reigning mandarins thus procure an easier access only a national one; other countries have long been attuned to its reverberations.

The result has not been entirely innocuous. The present generation of British opinion-makers are the intellectual *rentiers* of a more illustrious past. Banalities uttered in London, nevertheless, can still be projected with greater ease than pearls of genuine wisdom cast elsewhere. And that faculty serves to entrench the second-rate more firmly than ever, when for Britain only the first-rate will do.

Here, as in most sectors of British society, an "old

boy network" may smooth the path for some. But others can also be sped along it through the sort of coterie privilege that all collective undertakings tend to engender, on the Left and at the Center as well as on the Right, in an era of bigness. Those who refer to the Establishment are simply giving a local habitation and a name to the kind of power that organizational man, in varied groupings, pre-empts everywhere. American democracy is less classbound than British democracy but it, too, has an old boy network of its own.[2] In the United States, there is an unceasing struggle between economic forces that centralize the American power structure and all that, through the size of the country, keeps sectionalism alive. It is thus harder than in Britain to build up reputations or sustain them; thus, too, the manipulation of opinion becomes a more unwieldy task. Things must be done in Britain on a smaller scale. And yet that is how some can be made to appear larger than life, bigger than they are, with less ado.

This would not matter so much if it only enhanced the self-importance of intellectuals and public men. But their moral fiber can also be sapped by opinion-making facilities in which controls are so concentrated.

There is, for example, no alternative to the serious programs of the British Broadcasting Corporation. Among the serious-minded it has, as a result, a semicaptive audience. And that agency may corrupt by the way in which its patronage is bestowed or withheld. Journalists and editors, writers and scholars, get access to a wider public through talks and commentaries, interviews and reviews. They may, nevertheless, hesitate to intercede or speak out

2. Lionel Gelber, *The American Anarchy* (New York, 1953). Bigness and conformity was the theme of that book and it used the concept of "organizational man" some years before a best seller was to adopt it.

when BBC functionaries deny others, who are well qualified, the same resonant access.

But these are flaws. Against them should be set the fact that a political system superior to that of any other major country might never have matured in Britain if the British Isles were more spread out. Britain has been adept at making limited resources go far—a forte to which, apart from the native aptitudes of the British people, geography contributed. And now some may fear Britain is still overextended. She will not be overextended outwardly if she stretches herself inwardly as far as she can.

A middle stance between primacy and decline can, at any rate, be attained in this way and in no other. Nor is the regimen one from which any branch of national endeavor will be exempt. And this is a point which not all British intellectuals comprehend. In the study of world politics they praise each other for saying today what some in North America have been saying about international relations for two or three decades. Nor is it any wonder when Americans take the lead in the study of strategy and international relations. The levers of primacy in the West are American, and it is the experience with these levers that now counts most.[3]

One further comment on British public affairs is called for. When Britain enjoyed a higher rank, the best of her political thinkers could traverse a wide range of interests with authority and show the connection between them. Some still can. Yet on the great issue of Europeanization

3. Strategic studies are only one subdivision of modern history and international relations. There is a tendency in the United States for this one subdivision to overshadow the entire field. The application of the new war technology to general policy requires intensive, specialized research. "Make-work" in a few well-endowed quarters may also be suspected.

and Britain's place in the world, few of her political thinkers have had much to say. The question of British membership in the Common Market has been ventilated from various economic angles, but there has been no such thorough treatment for the problem as a whole.

Perhaps it was inevitable that specialists in one particular field should be heard from more and more—when, that is, the merely facile have not altogether taken over. There must be specialization. It breeds its own kind of insularity, nevertheless. Observers can be misled by the extent to which sophistication serves as a screen for the parochial, the unimaginative, and the ingrown. But statecraft is the art of seeing the relationship of things—and when Britain's status is being redefined, that is the sort of insight she needs most. She cannot always get it from intellectuals who have, as their *métier*, depth without breadth.

XXVIII   MUDDLING THROUGH?

Will the British people take themselves in hand? If they resolve to do so, they must select with care the things they can still do best, and it will be to their own detriment if they exasperate others by an outdated conceit— by the hypothesis, unexpressed and yet discernible, that they still know all the answers.

When this is believed by those who control opinion media, the effect at home is deleterious. Dissent may be foreclosed and public opinion thus manipulated with fewer qualms. Yet even the Comic Spirit must sigh on those leisure-class occasions when well-heeled British materialists decry American materialism.

A certain Palmerstonian arrogance among Americans

may be hard to take but, as an occupational disease of power, there is some warrant for it. Though there is scarcely the same warrant for it among the British today, many in Britain still betray signs of that tranquil consciousness of effortless superiority which Asquith, a Balliol man, attributed to his old Oxford college.[1]

Not that this is altogether a bad thing. It is better than the cynicism which erupts whenever the harsh realities of altered status close in. *De haut en bas,* nevertheless, is a posture which is more likely to invite shocks than soften them.

The effect of such traits may be considered from yet another standpoint. If the British economy had a forward thrust, they would do little harm. But it is across the

1. Balliol may now cut a somewhat different sort of figure with an ex-Communist as Master. It has long served the cause of a free critical intelligence in a free world order. These aims could not have been favored by its new Master during the many years he spent on the roster of the Communist Party. Politically he would have had to wink at hostile Communist activities throughout the period of the Nazi-Soviet Pact (when Communists in France and the United States aided and abetted the Nazis); for much of the Battle of Britain; and again, throughout the cold war, until after Soviet terror in Hungary late in the 1950's. Intellectually he would have had to accept Communist discipline during most of his professional career.

No blow is struck for the open mind when recent champions of the closed mind are rewarded institutionally. Mindlessness and muddle are given a bonus.

Balliol is not Oxford and Oxford is not Britain. But when a famous college disregards basic realities, one prewar observer is bound to recall how contemporaries, who later fought for King and Country, had declared in the Oxford Union that they would not do so. (A similar resolution was nearly carried again in 1965.)

Was the action taken by the Fellows of Balliol an echo of *la trahison des clercs*—a whiff of the political decadence which helped to corrode the moral fabric of Western Europe between the wars? It may only have been symptomatic, in an academic context, of a more widespread insularity—though even that has been a serious matter.

Balliol, at any rate, had raised questions that should have been discussed in major British opinion media—Left, Right, and Center. There was no such discussion.

The British people cannot always learn where and how they have been tying their own hands. Until these are untied, Britain may not fully play the part she should play.

Channel and across the Atlantic that free economies with
a forward thrust may now be found. And this is a contrast
in circumstances to which differences in atmosphere between Britain and the United States can be traced.

For more than a quarter of a century the United States·
and Canada have been going up in the world. Americans do not know what it is like, after being on top, to
make a sudden, cruel descent. Canadians have never been
on top and do not think in those terms. Americans and
Canadians, all the same, can perceive why there is this
difference of atmosphere and, counting their blessings,
make allowances for it.

Meanwhile, it is as a clue to British performance that
the temper of the British people must be gauged. Some
may contend that Britain's performance, taking the rough
with the smooth, has been no worse than that of others.
This could well be, and yet it is still disheartening.
Britain, in selected branches of endeavor, has to be better
than others. For her, if she is to play an important part
in the future, the passable is not good enough.

Neither friends nor enemies have conspired against
her on this score, though many Britons react as though
they had. Small in size, Britain has been large in scope.
Fate is what gave her a place in the sun that is *sui
generis* and, if she is to perform at all, she must perform
accordingly.

In other words, what she has to recapture are elite
standards that she herself once set. It was by a sound
instinct that the producers and distributors of Britain
were once wedded to elite standards. A number of them
still are; many are not. A drop in global rank has hurt
British pride. Pride now taken in elite standards would
not only soothe but fortify. These will have to be adapted
to a progressive mass society. It is only by resurrecting

them and spreading them more generally that Britain can hold her own.

And the hope that Britain will hold her own is one that allies and friends must nourish. They cannot write her off as her own Europeanizers sought to write off British overseas affinities during the Common Market campaign. Pillars of civilized society such as Britain are not overabundant. As a policy for Britain, Europeanization would be a counsel of despair. But no alternative to it will have a chance until the slipshod and sluggish are banished from factories and public services, until management (in training and methods) is more up to date, until there is more diligence in boardrooms at home and more zeal in British salesmanship abroad. The goose that lays the golden egg must not kill itself.

Britain might not be in a muddle today if the vain old superstition that she could always muddle through had been less popular during the first four decades of the twentieth century. World War II might have been averted if the British people had not overestimated their margin for error after World War I. Pre-eminence, however, was not in the nature of things; it could therefore be neither innate nor inert. What had to sustain it was not effortless superiority but superior effort.

Though the world has never owed Britain a living, many in Britain behave as though a living were owed them. In war, wrote Napoleon, the moral is to the physical as three quarters to one quarter; and, just as Churchill's Britain corroborated that maxim in a positive way, so, in a negative way, has postwar Britain. Excellence is the foe of mediocrity, but this only the wholehearted or single-minded can achieve. Without it Britain cannot get far.

3

AMERICA AND BRITAIN
Some Fundamentals Reconsidered

XXIX THE GAULLIST HERESY

When Britain was excluded from the Common Market,
the European policy of the United States went askew.
The United States had expected that American trade objectives could be pursued in one all-embracing series of
negotiations with the Common Market after Britain
signed up. This, however, was overoptimistic; another
series of negotiations may still be required—for reasons
not solely economic.

Charles de Gaulle felt that the needs of Britain and
of the Commonwealth countries could not be met without
the Common Market's altering its character. It was more
likely that Britain's status would have been drastically
recast upon entry into the Common Market. And Britain's
status could not be recast without a number of far-reaching issues being raised for the United States as leader
of the West. These issues cannot be neglected without
the free world's losing out.

In American assessments, a major role is still assigned
to Britain. That is why American laments over her ex-
clusion from the Common Market were so caustic. But for
Britain to play a major role, her economic sinews will
have to be toughened.

Britain does not stand alone. There are overseas countries that are attached to Britain economically through the Commonwealth; there are members of the European Free Trade Association (EFTA) who, if they could no longer take their cue from Britain, would have to look to the Common Market. The prosperity of these groupings serves wider political interests. But if it is to continue to do so, another bold, imaginative American initiative may have to be mounted.

Before anything can be done, however, the English-speaking peoples will have to put first things first. Confusion would be less rife if the crucial decision over entry or nonentry into the new Europe could actually have been registered by the British people themselves. As a representative democracy, Britain ranks high. But events did not permit her to make a decision about her own destiny, in full awareness, by herself.

And what would the British public say if it could? Despite a one-sided presentation by most opinion media, the majority view of the Labour Party has been against entry on terms Brussels would accept, while the Conservative Party has never been unanimous in its view.

Only a Swift or a Voltaire could truly depict the ironies of this bizarre conjuncture. An alternative to British membership in the Common Market is needed. In both London and Washington many have supposed that, with the eventual departure of General de Gaulle from office, the problem will be solved. They should know better. Personalities, amiable or not, have little to do with the case. The Europeanization of Britain is precluded by deep-seated obstacles that are largely impersonal.

The Commonwealth could not survive the Europeanization of Britain and neither, as a loose yet tested mainstay of the West, could Anglo-American friendship. In

British policy, the preservation of great historic assets must not take second place. Before Pearl Harbor, when the United States was still isolationist, the West was ill served by the fallacies of America First. Europe First could also do harm.

Overseas members of the Commonwealth may not always hold Britain to her trade pacts with them. Some might find other outlets for their foodstuffs; a few will become associate members of the Common Market. Short of actual entry into the Common Market, Britain herself should be able to make direct arrangements with it. There is, of course, more to the Commonwealth than trade pacts. But even if an accommodation over these trade pacts were reached at Brussels, that would not solve the problem. The political processes to which Britain would ineluctably be subjected are what, from the standpoint of the British role, must keep her out of "Europe." Upon those processes, a Gaullist incubus will not last forever. "Europe" must look ahead. But so must Britain.

General de Gaulle uttered no political heresy when he took his stand on this issue. All he did was put a governmental stamp on a conflict of interest within the West that had been perfectly visible from the outset. And the United States, as leader of the West, cannot keep aloof. What the conflict entails must be brought home to the American people if Washington is to join with vigor in the quest for an economic alternative to British membership in the Common Market.

One task that was shirked during the negotiations between Britain and the Common Market can be shirked no longer. Before the United States will feel obliged to mount a countervailing economic initiative, the political rationale of that initiative must be spelled out.

This will not be easy. A major role for Britain may be

an American postulate, but what if London and Washington differ over how that role can best be implemented?

Anglo-American vicissitudes are governed by a law of their own. There was an acute Anglo-American divergence, for example, after the Kennedy-Khrushchev encounter over Cuba in 1962, when the U.S. Defense Department canceled without notice the production of the Skybolt missile on which the British nuclear deterrent depended. Yet an Anglo-American reconvergence soon followed—with the Nassau agreement between President Kennedy and Prime Minister Macmillan, and General de Gaulle's veto of the British application for entry into the Common Market.

What might have done greater harm than a dispute over the type of British deterrent weapons, or even over their utility, was the move over which London and Washington had not been wrangling with each other but concurring: the outright participation by Britain in an integrated Europe.

Not that these vexed topics were unrelated. If Britain joined a European political union, she could not maintain a deterrent of her own. At the present time, while a British deterrent so closely linked with the American cannot be fully independent, it does at least symbolize an autonomous British role in other spheres. But if Britain became Europeanized, that autonomy would wane. And British autonomy could not wane without setting back American interests in many corners of the earth.

There was another angle from which to examine the issue. As long as France and China retained independent deterrents, it would be difficult for any government at Westminster to let a British deterrent wither away entirely. The British deterrent, however, has always been co-ordinated with the over-all American deterrent. It was to the independent French deterrent that the United States objected more strenuously. By the Nassau agreement of 1962, Britain had shown that, while she might assign her deterrent to NATO, she would not merge her deterrent with any new French one. And if Britain would not Europeanize her deterrent—this was a clincher for General de Gaulle after Nassau—she would not be disposed wholly to Europeanize herself.

Nor did it sweeten the pill for General de Gaulle when the Wilson Government laid further emphasis on NATO control of the British deterrent. Outright Europeanization was still withheld. It was in keeping with historic British overseas affinities that Britain should look beyond the new Europe. General de Gaulle made no mistake, therefore, when he saw that she would have to shake off those affinities before she could be, even in his own Gaullist, nonfederal sense, authentically European.

Lest Anglo-American interaction thwart him, *he* thwarted *it*. That was the real meaning of the French blackball at Brussels. Yet what does Anglo-American interaction itself mean? The French know—and dislike it. But how well is it known by the English-speaking peoples themselves?

XXX AMERICAN POLICY VERSUS AMERICAN INTERESTS

When the United States fostered the unity of Western Europe, she did not suspect it might actually *lessen* unity in the West. So, too, when Washington urged the Europeanization of Britain, it failed to perceive that common interests might be set back rather than furthered by such a move.

A free-world order would have been overcome if there had been no Anglo-American factor for upholding it at critical junctures since the turn of the century. But there would not have been this Anglo-American factor if the political independence of Britain had not always been presupposed by the United States, if American interests had not been fortified by Britain's geographical detachment from the European continent.

That, however, is not the way Washington now regards matters. The English Channel, in an era of nuclear weapons, no longer provides the seagirt Isle with a protective dike. Britain's defense problem is not, of course, hers alone—it is shared by her European neighbors.

Still valid, nevertheless, are some of the nonmilitary implications of Britain's traditional posture in world politics. These must have been overlooked when the United States adopted the Europeanization of Britain as a feature of her European policy. Though London and Washington diverge periodically, Britain is the one major transatlantic ally of the United States with whom some basic unison is most likely to endure.

In Anglo-American friendship, enemies of the free world have long detected an enemy of their own. They are right to do so. Prior to General de Gaulle, no figure of comparable stature in the West ever took the Anglo-American factor amiss. And thus it was in strange company that so eminent a champion of the French patrimony found himself. The Tsar Nicholas II railed against Anglo-American friendship before he aligned himself with Edwardian Britain. During the formative years of the Anglo-American factor, the German Emperor, William II, did what he could to disrupt it. Anglo-American friendship had much to do with bringing down that monarch's political heir, Adolf Hitler. Stalin and his successors ran up against the Anglo-American factor. And yet when

General de Gaulle did this, too, he did not have the same goal as any of those others. Many of his British and American critics, pursuing the Europeanization of Britain at any cost, were prepared to trifle with the Anglo-American factor. General de Gaulle—such were his prepossessions—had to steer clear of that factor entirely

In the resurrection of the term "Anglo-Saxon," even the language of Gaullism was reminiscent of a vanished epoch. For General de Gaulle blinked at the varied origins of the English-speaking peoples—not only in Britain and the United States, but in Canada, Australia, and New Zealand as well. Anglo-American relations, after all, were at their worst during the eighteenth and nineteenth centuries, when the British and American peoples seemed ethnically most akin, when ties of blood might have counted most. But later, what actually counted most was a common stake in a free-world order and an aptitude for preserving it in common. Anglo-American friendship became a major factor in world politics at a time when the United States was becoming less Anglo-Saxon than ever. That is the evidence of history, and even those who *make* history should pay heed.

At the turn of the century, there were some on both sides of the Atlantic who thought of Anglo-American friendship in vaguely racist terms. Most of those in Britain and the United States who were inclined this way were harmless in their inclinations. Among the French on the other hand (during the boyhood of Charles de Gaulle), a sinister pre-Nazi racism came to a head with the Dreyfus Case.

There was none of this in General de Gaulle himself. Yet his foreign policy, with its alternations between the archaic and realistic, did more than invoke the spirit of past centuries when France stood first in Europe; also brooding over Gaullist policy was the shade of the *fin de siècle*. When the contemporaneous effect of Anglo-American friendship kindled his wrath, and he derided American leadership, General de Gaulle knew what he was doing. His antagonism was a conscious one. But his use of the term "Anglo-Saxons," that quaint sardonic lapse into the language of a bygone era, sprang from the subconscious.

Meanwhile, Britain cannot renegotiate entry into the Common Market without many branches of American policy's being affected.

The broad political consequences of British membership should be brought out into the open. But official Washington, like official London, had more than economics in mind when it proposed a lowering of tariff barriers during the Common Market campaign.

The American program has been a threefold one. First, there would be a direct attempt to reach a trade agreement with the Six and others. Second, if Britain joined the Common Market, its autarchic tendencies might be checked from within; British experience as world trader and world banker would thus come in handy. Third, to cap these endeavors would be a close Atlantic partnership that would be political as well as economic in effect.

Reducing discrimination by the Common Market against American trade, this threefold program might also curb anti-American excursions in other fields. That, too, is why Washington has laid so much stress on British entry. With Britain as an integral part, it would be harder for the new Europe to strike out on its own.

All this is a far cry from what used to be said across the Atlantic about the British role in Europe. The iniquity of British efforts to divide and rule, the wickedness of "balance of power politics" was a constant refrain among American isolationists until Pearl Harbor.

Nor did that refrain expire at once. If its echoes had not lingered on, Winston Churchill might have had less to contend with when the further conduct of the war had to be planned with President Roosevelt and when a postwar settlement in Europe and Asia had to be discussed with Stalin. There could, however, be no American leadership without the exercise of power, and the sort of charge that Americans had been wont to level at Imperial Britain was to be leveled at their own country after World War II.

The recovery of Europe owed much to a better grasp of power realities in postwar Washington. And yet with that recovery has come a leadership problem not only for the United States but for those lesser European countries which have also feared the kind of lead that might emerge from within Western Europe itself. Their fears would be allayed, however, if there were a British stabilizer to keep the new Europe on an even keel. Domination by either France or West Germany—or both—is not a state of affairs that the Belgians, the Dutch, the Luxemburgers, or the Italians would relish. Nobody can foresee what post-Gaullist France will be like, how adamant will be the attachment of the Bonn Republic to the West, and how far to the Left Italy will go. Weaker members would therefore feel safer in a European union that had Britain as an integral part. But wider considerations decree another role for Britain, and these must prevail.

Not that a deaf ear should be turned to neighbors who ask Britain for support. There are, however, two points for them to recall. The first is that whatever serves the West in general also serves them. The second is that a great deal of the weight Britain might still exert as a

European Power must still derive from residual non-European sources of strength. Britain may do more to stabilize Western Europe if she can draw on these sources of strength than if, on being Europeanized, she has to let them run dry.

The problem would be less disconcerting if Britain could retire into her own shell and, like Sweden or Switzerland, allow the main burdens of world order to rest wholly on other shoulders. But what suits lesser neutrals will not suit a small island in the North Sea with a much bigger population, a Welfare State to be financed, improved mass living standards to be sustained, and an important part still to be played in European and world politics. Over the continuance of British influence across the Channel, official London and official Washington have been at one with each other. Yet that will do no good if prerequisites for its continuance are slurred over.

Vagaries on this topic are not inexplicable. When autocracies operate abroad, they try to deceive others; democracies are subject to self-deception. But in their approach to the new Europe, British and American policy-makers may have been actuated by motives they could not cheerfully avow. Hence their ambivalence. What prompted Europeanizers among the British was the conviction that the British would run the show. And American hopes that the British would do so stemmed from distrust of precisely those European trends that Washington itself had long been fostering.

XXXI THE UNITED STATES AND THE
EUROPEANIZATION OF BRITAIN

After Britain had been debarred from the Common
Market, negotiations for a political union were halted
again—even for one as limited as General de Gaulle had
envisaged. The very existence of the Common Market
has been jeopardized by other disputes. But as the Market
does carry on, it must contain and canalize the economic
pressures it is building up within itself. To get the most
out of the Common Market, there must be tools of governance in which supranational devices will tend to pre-
ponderate more and more.

Could an integrated Britain have been extricated from
a drive toward supranational devices, one that the self-
generating mandates of European integration will progressively speed up? She could not. That was so because,
with her economic autonomy reduced by membership, the
gravitational pull of the Common Market would have
proved irresistible. And none should have realized this
more fully than the Americans. Why did they keep mum?

In endorsing the close integration of Western Europe,
the United States was more European than the Europeans. And yet she herself is the chief example of how
centralizing impulses take over when the dynamics of
bigness hold sway in a large territorial expanse. In the
loose-knit American economy of the nineteenth century,
there had to be a Civil War before State rights could be
subordinated to an over-all federal sovereignty. There is
no analogy between centralizing impulses in Western
Europe today and those over which Americans shed
blood more than a century ago. But while integration can

be achieved by a number of methods and under a variety of tags, its political consequences would be much the same.

These did not come as readily within the ken of the British people. A continental environment has been the mold for American politics, while Britain has had an oceanic complex for making her mark. Free countries as vast as the United States, Canada, and Australia might never have attained national unity without some federalizing machinery. The British have conferred federal systems on others. The tight little isle has not had much firsthand experience with the theory and practice of federalism.

The British people now have a breathing spell in which to ascertain what Europeanization might have in store for them—to learn how Procrustean would be the effect of a federalizing process upon Britain's capacity in Europe and overseas. Americans could have enlightened them about this. But while the Americans were thinking strategically in global terms, they were not schooled to the overseas prerequisites of the British role. In a scheme, moreover, that foreshadowed a United States of Europe, the United States of America saw a projection of the American idea and, until of late, liked what she saw. At the same time, nevertheless, Washington sought a British safeguard within the prospective European federation. And it did so because, in American endeavors, doubt and faith have been commingled.

One problem, that of the two Germanies, has done most to breed ambiguities in the European aspect of American policy. Nowadays, the European balance of power is but a key segment in a global balance on which a free-world order reposes under American leadership. This free-world order would be undermined if West

Germany sold out to the East. It was as a bulwark of the West that the West promoted the Bonn Republic. The Bonn Republic could not cease to be such a bulwark without the global balance shifting against the West.

German reunification under Russian auspices: that was the danger that close bonds between France and West Germany were forged to prevent—though, even if the two Germanies were reunified under the auspices of the West, France would be dwarfed, cowed, and tamed. Through the European Communities, these Franco-German bonds might be drawn still tighter. But can Western Europe be consolidated without wider Atlantic bonds also being loosened?

There have thus been two alternate hazards, and it was for checking them both that the Europeanization of Britain would have been so expedient in American eyes. An integrated Britain could have backed France if the West Germans rebelled against the West. Conversely, she could have backed the United States if a European Third Force tried to seize the leadership of the West or tried to go it alone under French and West German guidance. General de Gaulle knew the size of the American stake in the West European sector of the global balance; only by underestimating it could he assume that all American troops might be withdrawn from Western Europe. Long before that comes to pass General de Gaulle will have departed, and France herself may be caught in the throes of yet another *bouleversement*. But could an integrated Britain render NATO Europe better service than a Britain that had not been integrated?

The answer must again be that Britain can do more in Europe when she has affinities that stretch beyond Europe. It is clear, nevertheless, that new ills have emerged with the recovery of Europe and precautions will have to be taken against them. But these should not be overdone—especially when other sectors of the world front also have claims.

A vital zone of Western defense would crumble if Moscow lured the Bonn Republic away from the West. And there was a time when Russia might have let East Germany out of her clutches if, when the two Germanies formed a greater Germany, the new Reich was neutralized. But such are the prospects in East Asia (with China on the march) that the status quo in Eastern and Central Europe is what the Soviet Union must now want to maintain.

When it does, moreover, the interests of the West are also served—though this is a truth long dodged by policymakers and opinion media on both sides of the Atlantic. It is, all the same, upon the German status quo that the economic and political future, as well as the military defenses, of the new Europe have been predicated. The Common Market is Western in orientation. But never would Russia have allowed a new Reich to emerge that might augment the strength of the West. And yet, by its sheer predominance, even a Reich that is pro-Western would be bad for the new Europe. Without its German segment the Common Market will have miscarried. It has, nevertheless, been only through a divided Germany that the Common Market can have a German segment which is pro-Western—one which can be oriented toward the West. Russia may insist upon the German status quo for reasons of her own. On no other basis, despite all that is said by its own movers and shakers, can the Common Market proceed.

It may be that, through NATO and the European Communities, a West German defection from West to East has in any case been forestalled. A Paris-Bonn axis, on the other hand, could have a Third Force as its upshot. General de Gaulle might have had more success with the Paris-Bonn axis if Bonn did not lean on American sponsorship of German reunification. Should Washington ever cool off, it might be possible to resuscitate the idea of a Third Force on French terms. Yet how far can a Third Force get? While it might fragment the West from within, it could not retire from the camp of the West entirely. Against elements that may fragment must be set factors like Anglo-American friendship that bind together. The function of the latter will have to be reevaluated. Divisive elements must be canvassed first of all.

XXXII HEGEMONY FOR WHOM?

The policies of allies must be assessed by global criteria when a world balance has to be preserved. The range of American responsibilities since World War II has been so extensive that American national interest has often had to be restated in global terms. Gaullist France, on the other hand, was rendered secure by a world balance that others upheld. A more self-regarding concept of national interest could therefore safely impel her.

The French have not been altogether frank about this. A nuclear deterrent, enabling France to assert herself on all levels, could be built only by skimping preparedness in other fields. The French argued that large-scale conventional warfare was outmoded. This rationalization allowed France to invoke national pride while doing less than other major allies for NATO, for the land defense of the West European sector of the global balance—a French national interest as vital as any.

Then there was South Vietnam, where the United States found Gaullist diplomacy so unhelpful. Communist China may have to be brought into world councils if a local agreement is to be worth more than a scrap of paper. There will, however, still be few means on the spot for enforcing a standstill in Vietnam. And Paris expected to influence Peking through a wider approach. A rapprochement between Washington and Moscow could deepen Peking's isolation. Yet Paris and Bonn might also oppose such a rapprochement until their own prior conditions, national and regional, are met. There is the old maxim that the enemy of my enemy is my friend— and a posture of dissidence is one that dissidents, East and West, may share. But there is even more that these very dissidents do not share. Gaullist France may have tried to extend her European policy to East Asian affairs. Whatever eases matters for Communist China could make the independence of weaker Asian neighbors even less tenable. And that could not happen without further impairing the East Asian and Southeast Asian sector of the world balance—a balance to which France also is indebted.

Gaullist France must have seen how Asian and European theaters were interconnected. But while European objectives governed French policy, the United States had a world policy to conduct. Here again, it was an underlying asymmetry, rather than the personal antipathies of General de Gaulle, that most Western capitals had to conjure with. European objectives might have caused Paris to move closer to Peking. But after hostilities mounted in Vietnam, European objectives might also have called—quite apart from the situation in Central Europe—for an early renewal of Franco-Russian ties.

During the Korean War and its aftermath, Britain

was anxious lest Soviet intimidation of Western Europe follow an American overinvolvement in East Asia. What Gaullist France might have feared was an American over-involvement in East Asia before the French deterrent had been completed. Timing was all. There can be no Gaullist Third Force unless and until the American presence in Western Europe is withdrawn; but neither can there be one if the Soviet Union reaps an unexpected windfall across the length and breadth of Europe as the result of a premature American withdrawal. Such a contingency may never occur. But if it does, a Franco-Russian entente today might stand France in good stead tomorrow.

In Latin America, the prospects are not the same. Soviet missile bases erected on Cuban soil might have subjected the United States, that stronghold of the free world, to the deadliest strategic blackmail. Cuba is still a point of departure for subversive activities among other Latin-American peoples. Unlike Asia, however, the area is one in which geography favors the West even though anti-American sentiment handicaps the United States below the Rio Grande. Gaullist France attempted to cash in on this, but from Washington's own standpoint, that was not wholly disadvantageous. An anti-American sentiment that took a pro-European guise was better than one by which only Moscow or Peking could profit.

Yet when the arena was as wide as the earth, it was not merely the ends of Gaullism that should have been measured by a global yardstick. So should the means. And here France fell short. The nation-state remained the prime Gaullist vehicle for the reconstruction of Europe. But among countervailing structures of global power, larger groupings were what swayed the course of events. France alone could not muster the required strength. And while a European Third Force embodied

Gaullist ideas, substance for a Third Force would have to come from that closer European integration which General de Gaulle rejected. Gaullism, by derogating from the unity of the West, harmed others. With a reach exceeding its grasp, it did little for itself.

This is not to disparage Gaullism unduly, or to contend that it burst forth unprovoked. The French cannot indict others for the ineptitude with which their own politicians and generals prepared for another war with their German neighbor as the Nazi threat grew. And yet the ignominy of France from 1940 to 1945 might have been averted if the English-speaking peoples had understood the position of France after 1919. But it is also true that if the French after 1945 had understood the position of the English-speaking peoples, the Western alliance might not be so badly split.

Not that the English-speaking peoples always understood their own positions. The Suez imbroglio of 1956 showed the depth of the misunderstandings that still yawned between Britain and the United States. France and Britain were coupled in the Suez venture. After the United States torpedoed that venture, West Europeans had less faith in American leadership and, hurrying to sign the Treaty of Rome by which the Common Market was established, were more and more disposed toward some fuller union. Yet Anglo-American reconvergence, as the unsurprising sequel to Anglo-American divergence, must have confirmed any doubts harbored by General de Gaulle about British help in detaching Western Europe from the United States. His veto on British entry into the Common Market was, after all, no sudden impetuous whim. To detach Western Europe from the United States, to have it stand on its own feet, was his purpose. But if it was better for the

West when he missed the mark, it was also better for the French.

In domestic affairs, under a shelter of power furnished by allies, Gaullist tactics were masterly. Yet they could not be more widely exercised without weakening the very shelter that made France secure. Though General de Gaulle spoke like an Olympian he did not always act like one. There was nothing fortuitous, in the light of history, about the origins of Gaullism. But history, in the light of current realities, passed it by before it even arose.[1]

In a Third Force, two paradoxes could be manifest. The first of these is that a Third Force would be unable to challenge the leadership of the United States without the global and regional balances that American power underwrites. Without those balances a Third Force could not gamble on an accommodation of its own with the Soviet Union. Secondly, while France might preen herself on being senior partner, it would not be France but the Bonn Republic that would gain the most.

General de Gaulle opposed the subjugation of non-Soviet Europe by either of two foreign hegemonies—the American or the Russian. His goal, of course, was the hegemony of France in non-Soviet Europe. But a German hegemony might have been what the French themselves, self-destructive as ever, would have brought about. As between American leadership and German reunification, has the advent of a greater Germany now become the lesser evil? In the Gaullist view, American leadership was

1. In this respect a parallel could be drawn, perhaps, between such outstanding politico-military personalities as General Douglas MacArthur and General Charles de Gaulle. The one acquired overweening self-confidence as a commander and proconsul, the other as a student of war and national leader. An intensiveness of outlook brought them both to the fore. And they were unsuited by it for problems of state-craft that occur nowadays on the most extensive of scales.

an evil to be combated at once. Though German reunification might ultimately be the greater evil for France, it was an issue that still waited in the wings.

NATO has incorporated safeguards against the recrudescence of an historic, free-wheeling German militarism. When, therefore, France impairs NATO in the name of French nationalism, she again impairs her own national security. She also postpones a settlement between Russia and the West. For Russia objects to the reunification of the two Germanies as much as ever. The more the Bonn Republic takes the place of France in the councils of the West, the longer Russia and the West will be at cross purposes.

It was only with a pledge of German reunification that Gaullist France could have enticed West Germany into a Third Force. But could she have persuaded the Kremlin to redeem that pledge for her? The Kremlin may have toyed with the idea of an all-German reunification which (as Western Europe disengaged from the United States and Britain) would wrench the Bonn Republic from the ambit of the West and, by demolishing the European balance, would turn the global balance from West to East. But the Soviet imperium could not be consolidated economically and strategically if its East German domain were relinquished. As long, too, as Russia keeps an East German buffer in her toils, there can be no German frontier pressure for the reacquisition of the Oder-Neisse lands from Poland or of more distant "lost territories"—no panic at the reappearance of a greater Germany among the Soviet client States of Eastern Europe and the unforgetting peoples of the Soviet Union.

German aggression was what put the countries of Eastern Europe—Lithuania, Latvia, Estonia, Poland, Czechoslovakia, Hungary, Roumania, and Bulgaria—

under Soviet rule. It was also what put East Germany there. Under the peace settlement of 1919, the West, with Germany vanquished and Russia in chaos, backed the cause of self-determination for the smaller countries in between. But it could not enforce any rights for Soviet captive States when Russia revived after World War II and interference entailed a risk of nuclear conflict.

The East-West contest tended, moreover, to dim a further aspect of this same problem. Many Germans dwelt beyond the boundaries of the prewar Reich. World War II broke out when self-determination for all Germans could not be reconciled with self-determination for weaker neighbors of the pre-war Reich in Eastern Europe. This, nevertheless, was a historic antithesis that postwar allies of the Bonn Republic disregarded. Self-determination for most Germans, East and West, was what they plumped for. Yet the Soviet client States of Eastern Europe were also the former victims of a greater Germany.

These Soviet client States may try to obtain more freedom through contacts with the West, but they do not want to throw off Russian shackles only to have another reunified German Reich staring them in the face. And that is why in Eastern Europe it is a Muscovite overlord rather than the democracies of the West who still has the better card to play.

There is a school of thought which argues that German reunification can still be attained after a close European unity is achieved between countries lying on both sides of the Iron Curtain. Yet would an altered context make that result a more feasible one? Nationalism is what the process of any wider European integration must restrain, but it cannot be restrained by reconstituting a solid Germanic block in the heart of Europe.

The Common Market demonstrates how there may be some broader European regroupment when Germanic elements are separated from each other. No barriers to their reunion would be left, however, in any pan-European scheme. Then, too, when systems of government are so diverse, no tight-knit pan-European union can be devised overnight. How soon would the Russians, most of all, be ready to join one?

Until they (and many others) are ready, will German claims enjoy the priority they have had in the diplomacy of the West? Not that these German claims are all that might prolong the cold war or delay a durable peace. But, as far as they do, the peoples of the West and much of mankind elsewhere may yet demur.

The West demoralized itself between the wars when it overlooked the fact that what Germans deemed justice for themselves could be achieved only at the expense of non-Germans. In the post-war world the German status quo—the division rather than the unification of the two Germanies—denoted a compromise between German rights and the rights of others. Compromise is the one basis on which a fair solution can be visualized.

There has been ample precedent for it. The French, the Walloons of Belgium, the Gallic Swiss, the Americans, and the Canadians do not feel that all who live next door to each other, speak the same tongue, and have common ethnic antecedents, must be joined together nationally. Nor did the Prussians when Bismarck evicted the Austrians from Germany. But many in the West were prepared to swallow a racist pretext when the Nazis seized Austria in 1938 and then crushed the Czechoslovak democracy on behalf of Sudeten Germans. Nowadays, when Sudeten and similar claims are revived, West Germans repudiate the methods of pan-Germanism.

What *should* be renounced is the entire objective of a greater Germany.

This, however, is more than the West demands. Memories are short. The peacemakers forbade an *Anschluss* between Germany and Austria after World War I. In no other way could the West preserve the peace settlement. Hitler, all the same, strode into Vienna with impunity and, as the West had let the European balance of power be demolished, the stage was set not only for Munich but for the Nazi-Soviet Pact, for World War II, and for the East-West contest that has been its sequel.[2]

Today, when Soviet and Western guarantees uphold the independence of neutral Austria, an Austro-German *Anschluss* would have to have the consent of both camps. But the West has given its consent in advance to another sort of *Anschluss*—that reunion of the two Germanies, which would again unsettle the power balance and bring dire consequences.

Violence is not all that West Germans must rule out. Any détente between Russia and the West will rest on a power balance which takes the division of the Germanies as its premise. Other peoples over the years have had to accept a change in their status. The general interest ordains that Germans, East and West, do so as well.

The idea of German reunification under Russian auspices has often been mooted; but Russia herself could be disquieted by a Third Force of which a greater Germany might soon be master. The Soviet Union can purchase the neutrality of a Third Force, but its docility, if

2. "Britain and the European Balance" was the title of an article by this writer which was published in London prior to the Austro-German *Anschluss*. It warned that the then current trends in British policy might have a Nazi-Soviet Pact as their result. Details may be found in a footnote on Page 63 of this book.

the chronicles of the past are any guide, would be less certain.

Russia, moreover, now has a Chinese thorn in her flesh. It may have been the Kremlin's intention, after Khrushchev's downfall, to placate Communist China. But the cracks could not be papered over when differences ran so deep. And the strain would not be lessened by the debut of a Third Force, one that might play off East against West on the Soviet rear in Central and Western Europe. A new Europe that puts a spoke in American wheels (and in those of countries like Britain still aligned with the United States) could further Muscovite designs. A Third Force that might embarrass Russia would be less welcome.

The progenitors of a Third Force may hope to outsmart the United States. They might only outsmart themselves. They may try to head off a Russo-American deal at their expense by making a prior deal with Moscow. But what would Moscow get out of one? A European Third Force might induce a grave shift in the global power balance against the West. But could Russia, with China to distract her, take full advantage of it? If she could not, an accord with the United States is still what the Kremlin must want most.

Sino-Soviet friction is there to be exploited. No European union, however, could exploit this safely by itself; it would have to have American security guarantees even while it attempted to outflank American leadership. These guarantees would not be needed if a European union could be a principal in the world contest. But it cannot be that as long as its own security must be underwritten.

If Russia, on the other hand, is ever to reinsure herself in the West, it is with an American principal that she must come to terms. (By the same token, since Russia rather than China is the other major nuclear Power, it is with her that the United States must first come to terms if the arms race is to be curtailed and the more imminent perils of the epoch allayed.) A Third Force, seeking a deal with Moscow, may bypass Washington. Moscow, seeking a deal with Washington, may bypass a Third Force.

War on two fronts—with the repetition of Bismarck's famous nightmare—was what spelled the doom of the German Reich, and Russia again has two fronts to watch. Short of a nuclear holocaust, the Soviet Union might not be able to break through the countervailing defenses of the West; that is what the Berlin crisis of 1961 and the Cuban crisis of 1962 revealed. The alternative, when Russia feels insecure on her East Asian frontiers, may be a settlement with the West that will at least render other Soviet frontiers more secure. It is in such a larger Eurasian setting that the future of the Germanies must also be reconsidered.

A greater Germany would not make the Soviet Union feel more secure. Russian national interest has been put before a common ideology in the deep-seated feud between the Soviet Union and Communist China on the Asian frontiers of Russia. There is no likelihood that national interest will somehow be overlooked on the European frontiers of Russia. Moscow now has Peking to keep its hands full. The Kremlin will not with alacrity reinstate Berlin as the capital of an overbearing nearby Power.

The experience of two world wars gave the West a parallel interest in the division of Germany. The cold war eclipsed that. But now an existing equilibrium—within the West as well as between the West and Russia

—supplies one foundation for a détente. Only with a divided Germany can this equilibrium be preserved.

What price Germany? Must that dread question, though in a different context, be asked again in this day and age? Most of mankind will rejoice over agreements between Russia and the West that serve universal objectives. The partial nuclear test ban was one such objective. All-German reunification is scarcely in the same category. Nevertheless, there is a West German veto upon any settlement between Russia and the West which accepts the division of Germany—upon any arrangements by which the reunion of the two Germanies would be precluded. A license given the Bonn Republic to hold things up must, of course, be traced back to Russia's postwar intransigence. But the Bonn Republic could never have extorted this cosmic, irredentist *pourboire* if its fidelity to the West had been beyond doubt.

Such a West German veto leaves its mark on many aspects of Western diplomacy. Bonn does less than Paris to cultivate Peking, hinder NATO, or detach Western Europe from the United States; it extracts from Washington as recompense a renewed backing for reunification of the two Germanies. The West German veto, however, also received support from French and British quarters, though for opposite reasons. Gaullist France endorsed it so as to gain Bonn's approval for her own European aims. Britain expected to get stouter support from Bonn for British entry into the Common Market.

Harold Wilson's Labour Government did not at first have the same European objective as its Conservative predecessors. But it did want West Germany to purchase more British arms or goods so that Britain could still meet the costs of the British Army of the Rhine—and so that the Bonn Republic would not regret having joined others to support the pound sterling. The German issue is not one over which any government at Westminster would wish to upset NATO and Anglo-American applecarts.

Then, too, the British Left would have had to part company with the Social Democrats, their West German counterparts, if they opposed German reunification. This, however, is not as much of a problem for the British Left when the Social Democrats become less irredentist than either the centrist or right-wing parties. Under Willy Brandt they increased their vote and he advocated an "Austrian solution" for East Germany—one by which the victors of World War II would guarantee East Germany's neutrality. But all Germans, those of the West as well as those of the East, would have to observe the limits of that neutrality and Moscow may not trust them to do so. Russia may also reject this proposal because it overlooks the place of East Germany in the Soviet imperium and the degree to which the status quo in Eastern Europe is what Russia now desires to maintain. The idea of an "Austrian solution" cannot, moreover, make headway when most West German utterances are pitched in quite another key.

The Bonn Republic has reaped the utmost advantage from the East-West contest, and is poised to reap still more. By leaning to the West and yet holding the West to ransom, it has kept open the road to all-German reunification—which the West has been promoting, and against which, at the same time, safeguards have been sought.

Here is a feat worthy of Bismarck. The fact is that Adenauer, as a unifier, could not accomplish as much as the Iron Chancellor, but he had much less to work with. If Russia had not threatened the West, the postwar German comeback would have taken another shape. Even now Russia can spike West German guns by abating her own threat to the West. Russia herself thus prolongs an East-West tension on which others, such as West Germany, may batten. For the pursuit of power through ideology is still a pursuit of power and must be regarded accordingly.

The Bonn Republic will balk as hard as it can against any settlement based on a divided Germany. But it might be outmaneuvered by events. It has been able to intimidate its own allies with hints of another Russo-German deal. There will be no threat left in these hints if the Soviet Union prefers to deal with the West as a whole.

A German problem would remain, but it would matter less if it were relegated (for the first time since Bismarck) from the center to the periphery of world politics.

Not that the Bonn Republic, as the second wealthiest country in the West, would let itself be sidetracked without trying to buy off the Soviet Union with loans, long-term credits, and technical knowledge. Others in the West have also begun to supply Russia with these facilities in increasing volume. They think that liquidation of the cold war will be hastened by more unrestricted trade. The topic is one over which allies might bicker as long as nothing better than a limited détente can be achieved.

But here West Germans might have their own grounds for anxiety because more general trade between Russia and the West could dash their hopes. Bonn's gambit may be a somewhat exclusive economic arrangement with Moscow. But Russia is less likely to be attracted by Bonn as trade with others in the West tends to grow.

An alliance is in danger when its controversies are over ends rather than means. Even though allies break ranks to compete for trade behind the Iron Curtain, they have all had the same cold war objectives. But West Germany seeks something that others do not. And that is a difference which must not be glossed over. Only the Bonn Republic demands concessions that could impinge on Russian vital interests—and, by their broad effect, on those of the West, too.

Then there is the question of Communist China. Would Moscow change its mind if Bonn undertook to build up China against Russia? That is most improbable. West Germany has been trying to exert pressure on the Soviet Union through Washington. One reason General de Gaulle could not get Bonn's support for a European Third Force was Bonn's dependence on American support for West German aims at Moscow. Paris, on the other hand, made its gestures to Peking and, if West Germans did the same, they would have more to provide economically. The latter, however, are not in the same position as the French—one false step and Bonn might find itself farther out on a limb than ever. West German ambitions are not all that have kept Washington and Moscow apart. But the United States and the Soviet Union will both look askance at anything that fortifies the Peking regime. Washington has frowned on the German status quo. It may detect virtue in this if West Germany, reverting to type, overreaches herself.

Nor could Bonn be sure of Paris. French support for West German ambitions in Moscow has had as its postulate West German support for French ambitions in Europe and the West. But this last has not been forthcoming. Instead there was the project for a mixed-manned NATO nuclear fleet—one which disclosed how far Washington would go to outdo Paris as well as Moscow in courting Bonn. French willingness to influence Moscow on behalf of Bonn would be unrewarding. Another tack might be to further the cause of European settlement by reanimating (beyond trade, consultative and co-operative procedures already undertaken), the political tradition of Franco-Russian agreement.

This tradition could be reanimated without there being a Popular Front or Communist dictatorship at the helm in post-Gaullist France. Moscow was more averse to a NATO Nuclear Force than Paris—though, when all such schemes are shelved, the Soviet Union, unlike Gaullist France, may sign a treaty against the spread of nuclear weapons. But the French also have ties, old and new, with client States of the Soviet imperium. Yesterday, one common bond between France and Russia and the other countries of Eastern Europe was defense against a greater Germany; tomorrow there may be the German status quo to maintain. Russia and the West recognize the need for some sort of détente. A Franco-Russian accord could remove any Gaullist stumbling block.

The French would have to insure, however, that such an accord was kept within bounds. Russia may seek an agreement which fosters her own continental ascendancy, but this is not what the French will have in mind. Paris and Moscow might both have been opposed to the American presence in Western Europe (as well as to American policy in Vietnam), but despite "zones of entente," they are still more opposed to each other on basic issues. Nor is this point an academic one. A rapprochement between the West and the Soviet Union must have multilateral safeguards. There would be none for France if she subscribed to a bilateral accord with unlimited aims. The maintenance of a divided Germany is something over which Paris may safely concur with Moscow. But a further agreement for bidding good riddance to the United States would have repercussions that were more than local. And France could not enter such an agreement without soon getting beyond her depth.

It is the structure of power in the West that renders France secure and that makes the idea of a French hegemony in Western Europe so preposterous. France might stand between the two global hegemonies of the United States and the Soviet Union if unaligned countries would stand behind her. Yet why should they? The much-wooed neutralists take what they can get from East and West; they would get no more by adopting France as an honorary Afro-Asian or looking to her for leadership. And even if they did, it would not serve the permanent interests of France. No full reassertion of permanent French interests is likely, however, until a stable post-Gaullist regime has firm control of the reins.

The French and West Germans still have to settle down with each other—a piece of unfinished business that may retard close integration in the Common Market and yet render it more necessary. The Western alliance may have to be reformed, but it would be hamstrung by redistributions of power such as Paris and Bonn have wanted to bring about. That is why both may have to have their wings clipped—and why, if this happens, they themselves will be better off.

For West Germany there may be another alternative. Raging against the loss of her veto on negotiations between Russia and the West, she might avenge herself on her allies by stalking out of the Western camp altogether. She would betray the West if a greater Reich, aggrandized but neutralized, should spring from another Russo-German accord. And the Bonn Republic, by sulking in its tent, by toying with a lesser neutralism, could still undermine the defenses of the West—though not without also wrecking its own.

Representative democracy has been taking hold among West Germans. But no other Western people has so pernicious a legacy to live down. The German past is what sets limits to the German future. Existing power balances are an outcome of German behavior. And these are balances that the Bonn Republic itself must accept if it is to develop a mature concept of its place in the world. Germans long glorified war (and finally converted a cult of inhumanity into a political system) because they regarded themselves as exceptions to normal rules. Vestiges of that most tragic German fallacy have yet to be scotched.[3]

The Germanies had not been long unified when the Emperor William II tried to encircle others and then

3. One example of the extent to which West Germans still regard themselves as exceptions to normal rules was furnished by an address which President Heinrich Lubke delivered on April 25, 1965, over the mass graves of Nazi victims at Bergen Belsen. There could scarcely be a more incongruous site for a solemn denial that the German people, as a people, bore guilt for murders done in their name. Nor was it easy to swallow this disclaimer after the numerous trials of those who made German infamy possible on a continental scale.

But a persisting moral confusion does not stand alone. It is also evident in an inveterate political confusion. Herr Lubke admitted that the German people themselves must take much of the blame for the fall of the Weimar Republic. But when he also assigned some of the blame to the Allied victors of World War I, the President of West Germany reiterated propaganda against "Versailles" and reparations that was a prime cause of World War II. Here, on Herr Lubke's lips, were half-truths with which from the outset pre-Nazi Germans sought to reverse the verdict of 1918, which were used to demoralize the West, and which at home and abroad Hitler exploited to such monstrous ends.

No less reminiscent of the 1920's and 1930's was the silence elsewhere in the West which greeted the President's ominous remarks. It is the prayer of the West that a deep-seated heritage of self-pitying political irrationality will be overcome among the younger generation of West Germans. But it will not be overcome if the West, remiss in speaking up, makes no effort to keep the record straight.

complained that Imperial Germany was being encircled. The modern Reich was divided between East and West after the second such attempt. Germany herself set in motion the forces that keep her divided, and now there is no road back. Reconciliation with others is what the Bonn Republic desires. It will first have to be reconciled to its own fate before reconciliation with others can be more than skin-deep.

The West will not be able to accept the conditions of peace as Moscow defines them. There may be a limited détente, but there can be no durable peace as long as Russia still wages political warfare against the West.

It may, however, be beyond Russia's capacity to vie ideologically with the West and at the same time maintain her other interests as well as she should. No strain of this kind harasses the West despite the disarray in which it finds itself. The West's staying power, after all, has been an essential element in its power for peace. And yet the Kremlin must still try to compete ideologically if it is to conserve the potency of a doctrine by which the entire Communist system is impelled, though its own grip on the Russian people tends to relax as living standards rise. It is under the rubric of peaceful coexistence that the Soviet Union now makes a bid for mastery abroad; insidious Western influences on the home front can simultaneously be fended off. But Moscow also supports "wars of liberation" against the West lest Afro-Asian militants look solely to Peking. Peaceful coexistence has thus been less than peaceful.

Nor could its Soviet brand be anything else. Even so, Moscow must have been taken aback when, as conflict in Vietnam revealed, an expedient designed to lessen risks only magnified them. A collision with the United States was, on the one hand, the last thing the Kremlin desired; the North Vietnamese, on the other hand, were sure to lean more and more toward China if Russia did not also back them substantially. Perhaps that would give her a better chance, when the hour was ripe, to offer counsels of moderation. Meanwhile Russian support for a "war of liberation" might involve Russia in a still wider war if she thereby allowed Hanoi rather than Moscow to make Soviet policy. And Moscow could not regain full control of Soviet policy without altering it.

It is reasonable to suppose that Russia will not want to prolong enmities with the West when the Communist Chinese, at once so multitudinous, so expansive, and so implacable, keep Russia's Asian frontiers on the alert. But Russia may fear that Communist China will outdo her among emergent nations if she liquidates differences with the West. Russia must have ideological weapons as sharp as China's if a more unruly Chinese version of communism is to be withstood. The West reacts when these weapons are wielded against it. When they are wielded against Communist China, the West is not displeased.

It is a vicious circle on a world scale, but one that may eventually be broken. Russia and the West cannot abandon the search for an equipoise within their own camps as long as they exert pressure against each other. But inner and outer change may be concurrent. In Eastern Europe, for example, a whole series of adjustments should be possible when the specter of a greater Germany recedes. Circumstances may impose a new scale of priorities on both sides of the Iron Curtain, and the effect would be salutary if they did.

These priorities can be sketched broadly here. Neither Russia nor the West desires China to exert an unobstructed sway over Eastern and Southern Asia. This means that anything which distracts Russia from Asian preoccupations, such as the re-emergence of a greater Germany, is not to the interests of the West. But if Moscow is against having a European power vacuum filled by a greater Germany, it may now be in the Soviet interest to have that vacuum filled by others. The United States, in conjunction with Atlantic allies, has filled a postwar power vacuum in Western and Central Europe lest Russia herself fill it. In a period of détente, it is better for Russia that such arrangements stand.

Moscow still demands, however, that Washington withdraw American troops from the West European sector of the global balance. And yet the Soviet Union can scarcely ask the West to accept the German status quo without recognizing that, from one end of Europe to the other, the status quo is of a piece—that if it is disturbed in Western Europe, Eastern Europe may not remain immune.

There is something else for Moscow to recognize: the West cannot make up its quarrel with Russia as long as Russia tries to upset the global balance by waging political warfare against the West. By the same token, the West will have to accept an existing power balance in Central and Eastern Europe if the Russian concept of peaceful coexistence should become genuinely peaceful at last.

In a world balance the repercussions of change would be world-wide. For a number of years before World War II, Maxim Litvinoff sought to bring about co-operation between Russia and the West against the Nazis. Not since the Tsardom, however, have Russian statesmen been regarded as top figures in some higher Establishment. During 1966, all the same, that is the category in which Alexei Kosygin found himself when he mediated at Tashkent between India and Pakistan. Nikita Khrushchev would have been able to undo the global status quo if Soviet missile bases could have been erected in Cuba in 1962. Four years later, thanks to the way John Kennedy remustered the countervailing defenses of the West, the global status quo had in Russia one of its two chief patrons.

Power realities have been telling their own tale. Under Communist doctrine, the Soviet Union had to act as an antagonist of the global status quo for half a century. But where the status quo must be prolonged, in the existing boundaries of Eastern Europe as on the Himalayan frontiers of India, it is not revolutionary change but the national interest which comes first. Can the global status quo be upheld in some quarters and undermined in others? Only if one presupposes that a piecemeal settlement between Russia and the West is possible. It may be possible over some questions. But the cold war would have been liquidated by now if that were so about all matters.

The contest between Russia and the West has been world-wide. Dimensions of any viable settlement must therefore be world-wide too.

The nature of such a settlement should not be misconstrued. For what may alter are not the forces in play, but the use to which they are put. The West, by its coalition diplomacy, has laid the groundwork for a détente with Russia—and power will still be required to press for a more durable peace. But traditional groupings, in spite of much that weakens them, will also still be required. It should be remembered that there has been no world crisis of any magnitude since the turn of the century that has not eventually pushed the English-

speaking peoples back into each other's arms. Scope for
Anglo-American friendship must therefore be preserved.

XXXIII THE UNITED STATES AND THE
COMMONWEALTH

There would be no place in world politics for Anglo-
American friendship if the line taken by London and
Washington during the ill-starred negotiations for British
membership in the Common Market had borne fruit—if
an integrated Britain had forfeited her autonomy and
abandoned overseas sources of residual strength. Store
has been set on Britain's role as a European stabilizer;
as such, she must have leverage for maneuver. She would
not have had this leverage if she had been wholly Europeanized as Washington urged. It would be one thing for
Britain to keep a free hand so as to help stave off either
a West German defection from the West or mischief
wrought by a European Third Force. It would be quite
another thing for her to be dragged in willy-nilly through
organic European links.

In her support of the old European balance of power,
Britain was once *la puissance médiatrice* and, with any
updated manifestation of this classic role as mediator,
organic European links would be at odds. Thanks to the
obduracy of Gaullist France, Britain may still retain the
necessary latitude. Britain can function as a European
regulator only if she maintains a certain detachment
from Europe. A synthesis of the European with the non-
European has been a clue to British statecraft in modern
times. Britain could not be Europeanized without that
crucial synthesis breaking down. And if it did break

down, the conditions under which British statecraft operates abroad would no longer exist.

The disruption of the Commonwealth was presupposed by the more militant Europeanizers among the British themselves. Its disruption would have troubled some in Washington even less.

This was shortsighted. As leader of the West, the United States should want all Commonwealth countries to prosper. Instead she waged a long campaign against Commonwealth trade preferences. Washington was as blind as London to the dislocations that would have followed if, as Britain was Europeanized, the Commonwealth had dissolved. The political consequences for all members of the Commonwealth would not everywhere have been the same, of course. Some would have moved more closely into the American orbit—not a circumstance over which most Americans would shed tears.

Australia and New Zealand have had their security against a renewal of Japanese aggression in the South Pacific underwritten by the United States. Today, with China on the rampage, Japan has virtually joined their circle. It is to Japan—as well as to Britain and the United States—that Australia and New Zealand are now looking for markets. No other Commonwealth countries have so cherished the British connection. But their public men have realized since the Brussels negotiations that they and Britain could soon be at a parting of the ways.

Then there is Canada. It is the very intimacy of strategic, economic, and cultural bonds with the United States that makes her chafe. Could these two North American countries be coupled together more closely without Canada's political independence being worn away? Commonwealth links have provided Canada with

a counterpoise against total absorption by her great
American neighbor. But if this counterpoise vanished, as
it would if Britain is Europeanized, Canadians would be
more hard-pressed than ever to maintain a national
identity.

In Asia and Africa, the Commonwealth could not
crumble without some of America's own global policies
being nullified. Commonwealth bonds may be fragile but,
from the standpoint of the West, they are quite
irreplaceable.

The United States, together with Britain and others
in the West, has spent huge sums to strengthen India
and bolster in that ancient land the British legacy of
parliamentary democracy. They may not succeed in every
respect and the Indian Army can yet take a leaf from
the Pakistani book. Neither military nor democratic governments would, however, return to the bankrupt foreign
policy of the 1950's—though India may secede from the
Commonwealth. The Commonwealth did not always enjoy Jawaharlal Nehru's esteem, but he rallied to the
Commonwealth during the Common Market campaign
and again when the Himalayan frontiers of India were
first breached by the Communist Chinese.

What made the subcontinent so vulnerable was strife
between India and Pakistan over Kashmir. India was
unaligned, but Pakistan, though armed by the United
States as an ally of the West, had put herself out of
favor through her rapprochement with Communist China.
Since the expansion of China is not something to which
Moscow will lend itself, Russia was as eager as the
West to have a stop put to the undeclared war between
India and Pakistan. Hostilities in Vietnam had suspended
the trend toward a détente between Russia and the West,
but the Asian status quo could not be preserved if India

was allowed to go under. That was evident in 1962, when the Soviet Union as well as the United States and Britain furnished India with aid.[1] It remains the key to the situation in Southern Asia today.

War on the Indian subcontinent has been a tragedy for each of its peoples, and the Commonwealth, with its two most populous members at each other's throats, has not escaped wholly unscathed. India now looks upon the struggle against her foes as a single conflict, even though it has to be fought on two broad fronts. And yet Britain, like the United States, will support India only on one of

1. At one late stage there was the possibility, raised by Nehru, of an Anglo-American air "umbrella" for the cities of India, while the Indian Air Force repelled the Chinese invaders. But three years later, during the undeclared war between India and Pakistan, London and Washington had to pursue a zigzag course.

In September, 1965, the United States and Britain withheld military aid from the two belligerents—a step which did much to induce acceptance of the United Nations cease-fire. When Communist China, backing Pakistan, threatened to launch a diversionary attack upon India, heed must have been paid by Peking to something said in a transatlantic broadcast by Harold Wilson, the British Prime Minister. Peking, he remarked, knew that the United States and Britain had made plans in 1962 and would help India if necessary.

In 1965, as a matter of fact, the Indian request would have been for American aircraft to take on the Chinese while the Indian Air Force dealt with the Pakistanis. This would have been a more far-reaching request than any submitted in 1962. And it is significant that New Delhi never contemplated making a similar request to Moscow. For, among all the surface realignments of the moment, the power foundations of Indian security were, at rock bottom, still what they had always been.

Strategic realities have been a ruthless chastener for India, as they once were—even more belatedly—for the United States herself. Gone are the illusions of *Panch Shila*. The question for India, as the Chinese produce nuclear weapons, has been whether she can afford to produce them or should accept nuclear guarantees from others.

Until the last days of Nehru, Indian neutralists usually found more excuses for the East than the West. Now, too, when India hopes that Russia will act as a regional counterpoise to China, it may still be inexpedient for India to acknowledge her dependence on a global equilibrium which, in conjunction with Britain, the United States has done so much to underwrite. But without this equilibrium, neither India nor Pakistan could ever maintain a national independence of her own.

those fronts—against aggression from Tibet by the Communist Chinese.

Delhi found the British attitude more disturbing than the American. When Washington and London halted the supply of military aid to Pakistan and India respectively, India had not only been procuring most of her arms from Britain but doing so through direct purchase. It therefore came as a shock when British shippers held back commercial shipments or when cargoes from Britain were unloaded at non-Indian ports en route. Supplies from Russia to India kept flowing without interruption.

A drastic reorientation is highly improbable. Both Delhi and Rawalpindi have tightropes to walk—the former between Moscow and Washington, the latter between Washington and Peking. But Rawalpindi and Moscow will not turn their backs on each other (as indicated by Kosygin's mediation between India and Pakistan at Tashkent). And as Rawalpindi and Delhi move to and fro, London cannot lie entirely off their beat.

India and Pakistan, at any rate, made their way to London after the Suez crisis of 1956. At that time, lest pan-Islamic solidarity serve the purposes of Pakistan, New Delhi had been playing up to Cairo, while Washington, Ottawa, and Moscow played up to Delhi. By 1965, however, London and Washington had long since been back on the same side of the barricades. India now accused Britain of bias, and as in 1956, there was again a cry for India to "quit the Commonwealth." Again, too, this cry revealed the extent to which other members still determined their attitude toward the Commonwealth by the course Britain followed.

It is this central role of Britain's that will decide the future of the Commonwealth. If India or Pakistan left the Commonwealth, the blow would be heavy—but not fatal. The secession of its pivotal British member is what would do most to break up the Commonwealth—and only the Europeanization of Britain would make her secession necessary.

An armed truce may be all that India and Pakistan can achieve as yet. If they do not batter each other again soon, attention will again be paid to their economic plight. If Commonwealth trade agreements were dropped by Britain or if the need for some wider American trade initiative was disregarded, India and Pakistan would certainly be worse off than they are.

The Commonwealth now serves as a bridge between the Occident and the Orient. Since the withdrawal of South Africa, Africans and Asians have taken this bridge more seriously. Its limitations are evident. If it had no mission, it would not survive., The East, at any rate, must envy the ease with which the West has access to a cluster of nations, as voluntary as it is unique, that cuts across so many frontiers of geography and culture, race and creed, allegiance and world view—one that, as a single entity, abjures power and yet which, by its mere existence, may even figure as an element of power.

XXXIV ANGLO-AMERICAN INTERACTION

Only through the *folie de grandeur* in Paris have London and Washington been saved from their own peculiar brands of folly. What they must now do is get Anglo-American interaction in perspective. When the political futures of France and West Germany are obscure, a high premium should be put on the recurrent scarcity value of Anglo-American friendship. Since the turn of the century, no similar factor in the defense of civilized

society has been so durable. But the conditions under
which Anglo-American friendship can endure must be
understood. If these conditions had been understood, the
Europeanization of Britain would not have been depicted
as a forward step, but as a step backward.

Journalistic comment, for instance, about Anglo-
American crises might with more perspective be less
doom-laden. Some wept, others rejoiced at the presumed
demise of Anglo-American friendship during the great
divergence over Suez. The corpse was bound to spring to
life again, and it did before long. In 1962, when Russian
missiles had to be retrieved from Cuba, it should have
been recognized that the American citadel cannot be
imperiled without the freedom of the entire West being
menaced.

Downing Street, with other European allies of the
United States, was quick to express support of the action
taken by President Kennedy. But the majority of British
opinion media did more to darken the view than to make
things clear.

The West would have been convulsed if there had
been a British veto in the Security Council of the United
Nations on the American naval quarantine of Castro's
Cuba. Such a step was, nevertheless, demanded by *The
Guardian,* a liberal British newspaper that has usually
been pro-American. It was mostly *The Daily Express,* a
right-wing, frequently anti-American, organ with a mass
appeal, that, cleaving to the heart of things, stood by the
American ally ungrudgingly. (Another Beaverbrook newspaper, *The Evening Standard,* did the same, and there
was forthright backing only from the two *Telegraphs*—
daily and Sunday—*The Mirror,* a tabloid, and the *Specta-
tor,* a weekly.)

Old Suez grievances still rankled in some British

quarters; in others there was the neutralist and anti-Western agitation of the nuclear disarmers. Yet no such political escapism could be in the national interest, and it did not last long.

Controversy over Skybolt flared next—Washington having canceled brusquely the production of a missile on which the British deterrent depended. President Kennedy and Prime Minister Harold Macmillan discussed the matter at Nassau. But that meeting came at a time when India was under assault from Communist China, when London and Washington had been making plans for some preconcerted action in support of India. The need for such preconcerted action speeded up Anglo-American reconvergence.

Nowhere more than in Britain should there have been appreciation of the difficulties faced by the United States in discharging tasks of a world-wide character. And nowhere, despite a variety of contraindications, was there greater sympathy. But Suez and Skybolt raised doubts in Britain whether American policy-makers realized how much a community of interest with Britain was in the American interest. Such doubts played into the hands of Europeanizers. The lures of "Europe," even for some who had opposed the Suez venture, were enhanced.

With divergence followed by reconvergence, Anglo-American friendship again ran true to form. It was agreed at Nassau that there should be a NATO deterrent with Polaris submarines. President de Gaulle turned down this proposal. The French deterrent was to be the tool of the hegemony of France in Western Europe and of Gaullist policy in the West. Nothing could divert her from building that deterrent. But, by rejecting the Kennedy-Macmillan plan, France excluded herself from those Anglo-American councils into which she had once

sought admission. She did so, moreover, because she detected in the Nassau agreement no death warrant for
Anglo-American friendship but an instrument for its
relief and renewal. Two thrusts against the friendship—
the rebuff at Brussels and the rejection of the Nassau
proposals—were directly related as separate moves in a
single French counterstroke.

General de Gaulle thus registered his objection to the
British phase of American policy in Europe. He also
saved Anglo-American friendship from itself. Yet the
Nassau agreement will be revised if an Atlantic Nuclear
Force, as proposed by the Wilson Government, ever sees
the light of day. For Washington had been insisting upon
its idea of a mixed-manned multilateral fleet. Unless
Britain took a large share in this particular project, it
would have been principally German-American in com-
position—a scheme, in other words, that would have
turned the history of the twentieth century upside down.[1]

The burdens of such an undertaking would be less
onerous if Britain could draw on her armory of other
weapons, if an Atlantic Nuclear Force consisting of more
than surface vessels was organized. The two projects did
resemble each other in one respect—both provided for
the American veto on the use of nuclear weapons. And

1. In Washington there was a lobby (with exponents in the higher
echelons of the Armed Forces and the State Department) for the Bonn
Republic to supplant Britain as America's chief ally. In nuclear matters,
West Germany would therefore have to be put on a par with Britain
either through some new NATO undertaking or by having Britain
dispose of the British deterrent. Here, again, American global interests
have been misconceived. While Britain might dispose of her deterrent,
the French in Western Europe and the Chinese in East Asia will still
possess theirs. Whatever downgrades Britain in Western Europe must
upgrade France—an eventuality that Washington can scarcely desire.
And elsewhere, too, neither Bonn nor Paris would do in conjunction
with the United States what Britain has long been doing.

so, while they might have altered nuclear arrangements within the West, they would not have modified basic disparities in nuclear control. But more immediate problems arose for the Wilson Government. In keeping with Party pledges, they were supposed to transfer the British nuclear deterrent elsewhere. Yet in a sphere as vital as nuclear defense, Downing Street could never permit existing British contacts with Washington to pass from London to Bonn gratuitously. And here Paris also entered the picture.

In contrast to the British attitude, General de Gaulle envisaged a political Europe that might be detached in military operations from its own American guarantor. (Even an Atlantic-minded "Europe" might try to loosen strategic bonds between itself and the United States.) No such aim would endear the President of France to Washington. And yet, while de Gaulle called for a political Europe, he himself shrank from those very federal institutions by which alone it can be made to work. The United States, on the other hand, fostered political Europe but shrank from the strategic consequences of what she had fostered.

A NATO Nuclear Force, subject to control by its European participants, might leave the United States with less control than she now has over the over-all nuclear deterrent. There have been moments when, in order to cosset Bonn or even Paris, Washington seemed willing to sponsor a scheme of that sort. But in practice, Washington under Lyndon Johnson has been as wary about the strategic consequences of political Europe as London under Harold Wilson—the American veto which was embedded in the British proposal for an Atlantic Nuclear Force having been borrowed from the earlier

American project for a multilateral, mixed-manned NATO fleet. Even Italy has desired the sort of participation that would come with co-ownership.

Pushing the new Europe ahead with one hand, Washington might thus pull it back with the other. But for Britain, these gyrations would not do. Established principles of British policy had to be reasserted.

An Atlantic Nuclear Force would accomplish much of its purpose without even taking form. Implicitly it might have debarred a European deterrent that would rest politically on a Paris-Bonn axis under French direction. Explicitly, it would also have headed off any attempt by the Bonn Republic, despite treaties, to build a deterrent of its own.

But a NATO Nuclear Force in its American or British version was not the way to quell or deflect an unruly Germanism. It might only have again bedeviled relations between the West and Russia (with her client States) at a time when more hopeful objectives were being nourished. And yet, until Russia dispels the suspicion that she might convert an unruly Germanism to her own use, the West may pander to that which both Russia and the West should abhor.

This may be one of those complicated problems for which there can be no perfect solution but which, if kept within bounds, can somehow be lived with. And here the new Europe itself might set a good example. Within the Common Market there is an innate federalizing tendency by which Britain's varied role would be hamstrung. She must therefore abstain. But the more West Germany, for instance, is unified with others, the less chance there is of German reunification.

Bonn's diplomacy may thus be self-fettered with the passage of time. But whatever fetters it, it could have a reverse, unfettering effect on general diplomacy. An ever closer union of the Six might render the fulfillment of German national ambitions ever more impracticable—and brighten the prospects for a détente between Russia and the West.

There has never been anything in Gaullism which forbade close military co-operation between Britain and France. Whatever those two countries do together has merely to further Gaullist designs. A tunnel may at last be dug under the English Channel; the opposition of British military authorities is now out of date.[2] So, too, "Concord," that inordinately expensive project for an Anglo-French supersonic plane, was undertaken as a civilian enterprise. And more than military co-operation may result from other aerospace programs between Britain and her European neighbors.

Behind such programs lies the inability of the British aircraft industry to match the high-pressure tactics of American competitors. These high-pressure tactics have had official backing—though the "NATO Common Market" in armaments that Washington proposed could repair some of the damage. But unfair American sales methods might also have presented some in Westminster and Whitehall with an unexpected opportunity. Europeanizers could now attempt to take fences by detour—to achieve, through an indirect functional approach, what might be achieved in no other manner.

A loosening of British defense ties with the United States could be the outcome—not a situation which would

2. There may, however, still be some in Britain who would use British consent for this project as a *quid pro quo* for French consent to Britain's entry into the Common Market. There are, besides, new and less costly means of modern transport. The more these are used, the more traffic can be shared by a variety of British ports and airfields. Nor is there any reason why Britain should pin herself down to a single cargo route, under the Channel, through France.

wring hearts in the Elysée Palace. Under suitable conditions, moreover, a London-Paris axis might still bring
around the West Germans. But would conditions be suitable? General de Gaulle wanted to detach Britain from
the United States—and there may be no need for post-
Gaullist France to grasp this same nettle formally. It
would still be under Gaullist rules if Britain thus entered
"Europe" through the back door rather than the front
door.

That, of course, is not how things are likely to turn
out. The Wilson Government found the cost of some
co-operative air projects too high; nor has the British
Labour Party been so avid for entry into the Common
Market that it would bear with Europeanization by a
fait accompli. British governments, Conservative and
Labour alike, may still enlarge co-operation among the
aerospace industries of Britain, France, West Germany,
Italy, and other European countries. This would be a
sensible thing to do if it had no Third Force undertones.
Such co-operation might in fact be used to usher post-
Gaullist France back into the center of NATO affairs.
No countries, however, have as many policies to implement in common as Britain and the United States. Arms
co-operation between their aircraft industries might be
coupled with political co-operation in underwriting the
defense of more distant theaters.

At the same time, any stranglehold on the British aircraft industry by its gargantuan American counterpart
would have to be averted. Much has been wrong with
the British aircraft industry, as with the way it has been
treated by Westminster and Whitehall. But if it can still
set the pace in British technological progress, it will give
a further lift to the British export drive and help Britain
keep control of her own communications. Lopsided ar-

rangements between the American and British aircraft industries would be to the disadvantage of the United States over the long haul, since Britain will function best when she is technologically robust. For Britain, joint ventures in production would be less costly. But research and development should flow across the Atlantic, as across the Channel, in both directions. Only Washington can ensure that such a flow is maintained.

New, wider fronts for an Anglo-American concert are opening up. It has been argued in these pages that pressure for Europeanizing the British people will be resumed when the time is again opportune. At odds with that pressure will be the need for Britain to meet fresh overseas contingencies in conjunction with the United States.

Such contingencies may arise East of Suez—in an Indo-Pacific region where London and Washington have had commitments to allies under SEATO and where a number of important countries are still associated with Britain through Commonwealth ties. These are countries where the industrial base is still relatively small, where national units have little sense of national unity, and where the West's colonial past is still held against it. India is among those upon whom Communist China, emerging at last as a nuclear Power, casts an ever-deepening shadow. The security of India, and that of others in the vicinity, may (with or without assistance from Russia) have to be reinforced.

The United States, Britain, and the Soviet Union wish to stop the spread of nuclear weapons. But the Communist Chinese will lord it over their Asian neighbors unless some adequate counterweight can be provided. Though Japan has the nonnuclear capacity to enter the nuclear race, she has been depending on her security pact with the United States. She may yet branch out on her own. India, on the other hand, has had assistance from Canada in equipping herself with nuclear technology for peacetime use. Lest she be crushed in a Sino-Pakistani nutcracker, she may produce her own nuclear weapons. During the emergencies of 1962 and 1965, Washington, London, and Moscow had shown that the Indians would not be without support against the Communist Chinese. That support would simplify but not entirely solve the problem of Indian defense.

Still less will India have solved anything by manufacturing nuclear weapons. For one thing, she cannot enter the nuclear race and still hope to alleviate the lot of her own people. Her experiment in representative democracy might collapse under the strain. And even if she did produce nuclear weapons without disaster on the home front, it would take many years (as it is taking China) to acquire the necessary delivery systems. For a safe passage through that danger zone, India may need conjoint guarantees more than ever. Nor is she the only Asian country that might be exposed to Chinese nuclear blackmail. The security of others in the region will also have to be underpinned.

Not that that can be done with ease. Russia, for one, could not sign a conjoint guarantee without a complete realignment—without moving from the side of her Chinese ally to the side of those who have kept the Sino-Soviet camp at bay. No such upheaval is in sight. As for India, she would have to forsake a policy of nonalignment if the only security guarantees she received were from the two main pillars of the West, if the United States and Britain proffered these but the Soviet Union did not. Nonnuclear states, moreover, have been loath to sign a nondissemination agreement until the nuclear powers, some of whom could be their own guarantors, also begin to disarm. From a military standpoint, it is not clear how the United States and Britain can implement security guarantees, nuclear and nonnuclear, in a semi-continental area as distant as Southern Asia from the Atlantic region. Nevertheless, the United States and Britain will do all they can to protect Southern Asia.

What this might entail for Britain, as well as for the United States, should be evident. Those who have no deterrent of their own cannot, on behalf of others, assist in the deterrence of China. The ability to enforce commitments (such are power politics in an air-atomic age) is what may render the enforcement unnecessary. But, if that is so, it raises a question as to whether Britain can do her job as a political underwriter without some or all of the nuclear tools that the job might demand. It may have been the objective of the Wilson Government to "internationalize" Britain's nuclear resources not only for Europe but in Asia. No safe way of doing that has been found to date.

But the unforeseen can still be dealt with. When Britain went to the support of the Malaysian Federation against Indonesia, only conventional weapons were deployed. That difference in approach should be noted. Variations on the same theme call for more than one kind of preparedness.

They also call for more than one kind of diplomacy. The political means must therefore also be diverse. The United States could not act alone in a matter of this sort without stirring up a charge of American hegemony among Asian neutralists. She might, however, dilute that charge by sharing burdens with Britain.

And, besides, it is through remaining British outposts that the United States might get better access to the huge arc of the Indian Ocean. From Aden to Singapore the old British footholds have been crumbling; though Aden is being relinquished, an attempt to hold the bastion of Singapore will be made. Then, too, a new chain of small bases might have a big Australian base as an operational headquarters for Anglo-American co-operation. It is one of history's many quirks that scattered remnants of the old Empire should now be employed for the defense of anticolonial former dependencies.[3] The British presence in these bases, Commonwealth ties, the mobility of British forces—all these, the Wilson Government pointed out, permit Britain to make a contribution toward peace-keeping in vast areas of the world where no other country is able to assume the same responsibility.

This concept of the British role is one to which the Conservative Party, with its Europeanizing line, no longer fully subscribes. As an alternative to a Western military presence in the Orient, it sees Asian and African countries acquiring a local equilibrium of their own. But until they can do this, how is the advance of Russia or China to be withstood? That poser must not be dodged. Since World War II there has, after all, been no local equilibrium that could by itself make even Western Europe secure. The United States has buttressed Western Europe, and she has done so because it is a key sector of a global balance. As much cannot be done for other sectors. Yet they cannot be wholly abandoned.

During the 1950's there were neutralist and unilateralist factions in the Labour Party that wanted Britain to

3. Though India sought air cover from Washington and London when the Communist Chinese had to be withstood, she still opposes the establishment of Anglo-American bases in the Indian Ocean. If she approves, Russia might take offense. But it is also to Russia's interest that China should be held at bay. Until a global settlement between Russia and the West can be worked out, some doctrinaire make-believe will linger in India's attitude toward the West.

renege on her commitment to the Western Alliance. A
similar flight from reality could be essayed by some in
the high command of the Conservative Party when they
sat on the Opposition benches.

Not that a Labour Government may long sacrifice its
social and economic program at home by undue expendi-
ture on British defense commitments in the Persian Gulf,
Malaysia and Singapore. But neither the Right nor the
Left can afford a rigid doctrinaire approach. It is im-
possible to foresee all future contingencies. There may
be many, however, that Britain will still desire to meet.
She will be unable to meet them if prerequisites for a
continuing overseas British role are, wishfully, inflexibly
and irrecoverably, now erased.

When the situation in Indo-China went from bad to
worse and the United States intervened directly against
North Vietnam, President Johnson had the support of
Downing Street. There was more than just the independ-
ence of South Vietnam and her neighbors to be preserved.
The global balance would be jeopardized if Communist
China could prey unmolested on all that lay to the south
and then lunge toward Australia and New Zealand.

Britain did what she could to avert that last contingency by shoring up the defenses of Malaysia against
Indonesia—with assistance from other Western members
of the Commonwealth. But when Washington asked for
token forces to be dispatched to Vietnam, only Australia
and New Zealand (apart from South Korea, the Philip-
pines and Thailand) sent them. British abstention may,
thereupon, have inspired some in Washington official
quarters (together with a Europeanizing nod among
some of the British themselves) to suggest that Australia
could even supplant Britain as America's chief ally east
of Suez. And Australians, who hitherto have let Britain

pay for the peacetime defense of their own Indo-Pacific
region, now expend more than they did on defense.
Australia's capacity, economic and demographic, must
not, however, be exaggerated. There was, all the same,
much in the Vietnamese situation which compelled British diplomacy to blow hot and cold.

Britain had been Co-Chairman of the Geneva Conference through which the French retired from Indo-China
and she now did nothing that would disqualify her when
a settlement of the war in Vietnam was negotiated. (Her
Russian Co-Chairman, in providing North Vietnam with
support, did not have to be so punctilious.) Such were
the grounds on which the dispatch of British troops had
been withheld and the sale of British arms had been
regulated—even though that sale of arms might have
helped to pay for the purchase of military aircraft from
the United States. Then, too, Malaysian preoccupations,
together with unrest in Aden and Southern Arabia, had,
at first, left Britain with no troops to spare.

Not that when she assisted Malaysia, this had been
the sort of undertaking on which a Power with straitened
finances might normally embark. But Malaysia contributed substantially, through sales of rubber and tin, to the
dollar earnings of the sterling area. When Britain came
to her defense, she was not merely warding off Indonesia:
Jakarta was hand in glove with Peking.

Singapore seceded from Malaysia and, while that important naval base has maintained defense ties with
Britain, it is now numbered among Commonwealth neutrals. Since the Korean War, the United States and Britain have not always seen eye to eye on the affairs of East
Asia—yet they have been thrown together there.

This Anglo-American line-up was expedited by a development which, despite Asian setbacks, has incalculably

improved the underlying global position of the West. President Kennedy failed to get a good press in Britain when he demanded that Russia remove Soviet missiles from Cuba. But, by 1965-66, thanks to his firm stand in 1962, no similar confrontation between Russia and the United States seemed afterwards likely to occur. There was clamor on the Left for Britain to wrest herself away from the United States when American aircraft chastised North Vietnam. The Wilson Government dissociated itself from the bombing of fuel depots in populated areas. But otherwise, with backing in Parliament from the Conservative Opposition, they held to their course.

By-products of American intervention in Vietnam could, moreover, soon be taken into account. For, through it, other Asian peoples might have been saved from early subjugation by the resurgent Chinese. This would not have brought solace to those among the Vietnamese who suffered most. But the sheer vigor of the American intervention in Vietnam might have caused Peking to cease and desist when China made her feint against India during the Indo-Pakistani war of 1965. It might also have emboldened Indonesian generals, with Indonesia blocked anyway by British forces in Malaysia, to remove their country from the Chinese orbit altogether.

The economic strain under which the huge, driven semidestitute population of China toils would be relaxed if exclusive access could be procured to the rich natural resources of the vast, misgoverned Indonesian archipelago. Thus, too, a series of steppingstones toward Australasia would be at Peking's disposal. Among the neighbors of China, only Russia could still resist her. The global balance, with most of its Asian sector under China's thumb, would have been weakened. London and Washington have wanted the status quo of Southern and

Southeastern Asia to be maintained. Action taken by the United States in one part of Asia might have paid dividends in other more crucial parts.

In East Asia there was no alternative to Anglo-American co-operation. When any in the West defend the liberties of Asian peoples, they also maintain the Asian sector of a global equilibrium. It is not Machiavellian or Janus-faced to serve a double purpose in this fashion. When self-interest and the common interest coincide, a policy has the best of all sanctions. In the old European balance of power, the liberties of small countries were preserved or retrieved when a Power like Britain resisted an overweening domination. Now the scale of things has been enlarged, and what it is possible to do in one sector of the global equilibrium may not be possible to do in another. The need for an Anglo-American concert is a fact which the weak, if they wish to be protected from the strong, should be the first and not the last to appreciate.

When the Rhodesian issue arose, Washington, in its turn, supported London. Britain hoped, through economic sanctions, to assert the elementary rights of an African majority against a rebellious white minority. As during the Suez crisis of 1956, Britain was again in the dock at the United Nations—though when African members of the Commonwealth threatened to secede, it was not because Britain had resorted to arms but because she had refrained, at first, from doing so.

The particular circumstances of Anglo-American solidarity at any one juncture are, then, not all that should be examined. These particular circumstances must vary. What will not vary is the manner in which, despite vicissitudes, the Anglo-American factor persists. History may or may not have a pattern, but something very like one can be detected in the impress laid by the Anglo-American factor upon its own time. The United States in her own interest should want it to continue to be as effective as possible. It cannot be effective if British sources of strength ebb and fall away.

Only the British people can perpetuate Britain's overseas role. Their task, all the same, will be a less onerous one if the United States does all it can to help Britain's capacity to serve common global objectives. This help should come in the fields of science and technology, in that of world trade as well as in that of international finance.

Winston Churchill, with more to recall than his own collaboration with Franklin Delano Roosevelt, talked about a special relationship—a concept that is now jejune and passé, according to skeptics on both sides of the Atlantic. A number of countries, they point out, have "special relationships," not only with the United States but with each other. While that is true, it is not, broadly, the whole truth. What may be special about the relationship between the United States and Britain is what these two Powers have done, and will do, in tandem.

This does not mean that the United States and Britain must always concur. But it does set limits to disagreements which, if overstepped, would rock the West. Washington overstepped those limits during the Suez episode. Because the United States and Britain have more extensive interests than any of their allies, the terrain for treading on each other's toes is more extensive, too—the occasions that much more numerous. What drives the United States and Britain apart is all that observers sometimes see. More illuminating is the way they are pushed together again through underlying realities.

A great deal had altered when the United States took

Britain's place as leader of the West, but the fundamentals of Anglo-American friendship have not. That is
why friction between the United States and Britain must
be distinguished from friction that has occurred with an
errant French ally, and that may occur more and more
with the Bonn Republic. Britain, unlike Gaullist France,
has accepted American leadership, by and large. Unlike
West Germany, Britain has no unsatisfied territorial aspirations that could protract the East-West contest or
through which, if the Bonn Republic broke away, the
West could be subverted and crippled. Anglo-American
divergences are quantitative rather than qualitative—differences of degree rather than of kind. But Britain would
have to go along with others if she was Europeanized.
Such a step would extinguish an Anglo-American poten-
tial. It would thus also finish off a factor to which free
men owe much.

A European makeweight to American primacy was
favored, all the same, by some British enthusiasts for
membership in the Common Market. One potent, if un-
publicized, feature of her great debate was the hypothesis that a role for Britain as first among European equals
might be less irksome than one of junior partner to the
United States. Those who put the emphasis on Europe
were outwardly in accord with American promptings and
proddings; inwardly, they were spurred by discontent
with American leadership. A Gaullism of their own had
in fact preceded the anti-Gaullism that General de Gaulle
provoked among them.

But could Britain, instead of keeping particularly in
touch with the United States, stand first in Western
Europe? For the British to exert strength in Europe they
must, as always, draw on sources of strength beyond
Europe. Toward the close of 1965 General de Gaulle

thought Britain would shortly have fewer of these sources at her disposal. Even he might therefore soon view the entry of Britain into "Europe" with more sympathy. Yet some months later the French were chiding Britain for her unreadiness, from an economic and financial standpoint, for membership in the Common Market. The political argument of 1963 might thus be hushed. But Britain's crisis must be looked at from quite another angle. The British people could stay out of the Common Market with greater ease if they took measures that groomed them for membership in it. For the underlying issues had not altered. They are, in the long run, unalterable.

Britain is both a European and an extra-European Power. And that is an axiom which, if she is to attain a middle stance between primacy and decline, she must never overlook.

XXXV AXIOMS FOR THE BRITISH

Where do we go from here? To this question the most constructive response should come from the United States. But the British must also take stock. These five subjects will have to be reassessed.

1. Britons and Americans alike must see the Commonwealth as it is. It is not an entity dwelling apart from Britain. Britain—a point often glossed over—is also a Commonwealth country. But the notion of a self-contained Commonwealth is illusory. Trade is not the only field in which a self-contained Commonwealth would be unfeasible. Defense is another. Most Afro-Asian members are neutralists, while Britain, Canada, Australia, and New Zealand, even Pakistan, have strategic arrangements

of their own with the United States. Commonwealth countries still have interests that overlap—and as long as they do, the Commonwealth may persist. But there is also an overlapping between Commonwealth ties and Anglo-American friendship. Not all concerned will regard these relationships as forming, in the aggregate, a single miscellaneous whole. Britain should do so.

2. It has been contended in these pages that, if Britain is to continue as hub of an oceanic complex, she cannot merge with a close-knit Europe—and that her continuance as hub of an oceanic complex is in the American interest. But the same argument—such are European trends—can be reversed. Britain, it can be contended, might persevere as a hub only as long as the West is led by the United States and only as long as the conditions for Anglo-American friendship, a prime element in American primacy, are preserved. These conditions cannot be preserved if neither Britain nor the United States realizes what they are.

3. When the European and extra-European interests of Britain are again blended, what certitude can Britain have that American forces will continue to mount guard in Western Europe? Here the global dimensions of the East-West contest are what must tell. If the United States does not do all she can to help maintain its European sector, the global balance will shift against her. And there is nothing in the Gaullist analysis by which these basic realities can be gainsaid.

4. What should be the attitude of the British when the United States takes action that is ill-conceived? Britons are bound to speak out—though among them, as among Americans, informed critics may be less sensational in utterance than the hostile or the naïve. There are circumstances that Washington, by itself, can do

little to correct. If British views are to have perspective, British opinion media and British public men must still distinguish between what the United States can do to redress disparities of power and what is imposed upon the United States by the new war technology, by the sheer exigencies of leadership. A strategic interlock that defends the West also puts it in jeopardy. The twentieth century is what produced this state of affairs. While the American people will assuredly leave their imprint upon the age, they did not create it. If the United States copes with current interrelated perils, all will be well. If she does not, she may find herself a victim of those perils as much as any and more than most.

5. Finally, an axiom that sums up and overrides everything: American primacy is better than any Third Force alternative. Even in the West, some beneficiaries of a free-world order have done less than others against threats of a Communist take-over. Among neutralists, there are those who believe that the merits of the United States as leader of the West are outweighed by demerits. Allies may feel that the United States as senior partner is far from ideal. The annals of the twentieth century, nevertheless, bear witness to the cardinal fact that an Atlantic world in which the United States comes first would be a more tolerable one for Britain and other free peoples than one in which the French and West Germans have the final say.

Though a tacit Anglo-American bond has been the abiding core of the West, the United States has occasionally shopped around for some alternative to it. Time after time, there has been nowhere but London to which Washington could turn and nowhere but Washington to which London could turn. It will be sad if both miss the crucial significance of those habitual reversions. If they

perceive it, they must not press again for a Europeanization of Britain.

These, then, are five points of the global compass by
which bearings must be taken in future economic negotiations.

XXXVI THE POLITICAL CASE FOR AN AMERICAN INITIATIVE

An integration that will revolutionize the life of Western
Europe has been easier to begin than to complete. It
may, nevertheless, be one of those causes that could
forge ahead overnight. Politics and economics are, after
all, inseparable. That is how the new Europe can make
a political impact before it has crystallized politically.
And even that early impact, from an Anglo-American
standpoint, may not be altogether welcome. What Washington and London must ask themselves is clear: is
Brussels, in default of any other, to become the economic
focus of the West? Would it not be better for all free
peoples if this were to be in Washington rather than
Brussels? And how can the United States lead the West
politically if she lets the new Europe rule the roost
economically?

Questions like these could never have arisen when
Europe lay prostrate and succor came through the Marshall Plan. The success of that great innovating American
enterprise was what again brought European countries
to the fore. But now the United States has to insure that
her own economic growth is maintained.

The American Trade Expansion Act of 1962 was the
first step in the economic sphere toward that concrete
Atlantic partnership of which President Kennedy spoke.

If any benefits flow from American negotiations with the Six, these will be shared by Britain, by the European Free Trade Association, and by overseas members of the Commonwealth. But what if it proves as arduous for the United States to negotiate an economic accord with the Common Market as it was for Britain in trying to achieve entry? The case is made more cogent than ever for setting other currents in motion.

Illusions will have to be shattered. Washington has regarded the Common Market as a steppingstone toward more universal trade principles. It may not be one. And if it is not one, another economic regrouping within the West itself will probably have to be organized. To make this possible, the General Agreement on Tariffs and Trade (GATT) must not show partiality toward the Common Market; GATT's most-favored-nation clause may have to be amended. What might best serve the aims of GATT is an economic regrouping under an American lead.[1]

Not that a countervailing American project would be to the liking of protectionist elements in Congress. Nor would it be child's play to procure an adequate degree of harmony between the American economy and the econ-

1. It was argued for some time prior to General de Gaulle's veto of January, 1963, that an American initiative would be required if Britain were to hold out and if even a limited American deal with the Common Market could not be reached. (Address by the writer before the Parliamentary Group, Commonwealth Industries Association, House of Commons, London, November 26, 1962, as published in the Association's "Monthly Bulletin" No. 260, December 1962.)

It had previously been suggested that Washington urge countries of the Common Market to make allowances, in the interest of the West, for British needs. (Article by the writer, *The Statist,* London, March 9, 1962.)

On the political case against British entry into "Europe," there were passages by the writer in an article in *Foreign Affairs* (New York) January, 1963. Also in *Worldview* (New York) May, 1963.

For a fuller analysis of the politico-strategic case for an American economic initiative, see the writer's article in *Orbis,* (University of Pennsylvania), Summer, 1963.

omies of the numerous countries—from Japan to Africa
and from the Middle East to Latin America—with whom
a new pattern of trade would have to be devised. Since
World War II, Congress has responded positively to
American Presidential demands. If the United States had
been less munificent, thriving components of the Common Market might never have been furnished with the
economic sinews of their own postwar recovery. And
now the demands of leadership may elicit yet another
initiative from the United States.

Can this be attained without the Executive's making
concessions which protectionist elements in Congress,
echoing their European counterparts, will reject? The
national interest, surely, is what they must wish to protect first of all. But the United States is leader of the
West and the entire West will be set back if allies do not
fare as well economically as they might.[2]

2. Washington expressed sympathy when Britain had to take emergency fiscal measures during the autumn of 1964. These could not
be prolonged without having a boomerang effect at home and abroad.
Beyond the British emergency measures and the snail-like Kennedy
round, the need may soon arise for Washington to wipe the slate
clean and start afresh.

As a reserve currency for the sterling area, the British pound is
used more widely in world trade than even that other reserve currency,
the American dollar. Members of an international consortium were
therefore helping their own economies when they came to the support
of sterling in November, 1964. One-third of the credits granted were
American.

It was typical of Bonn that only Dr. Erhard, the West-German
Chancellor, should have felt Bonn's financial co-operation entitled it to
a political *quid pro quo*—that he could now ask Britain for understanding of Bonn's position in the world. For the others, it sufficed
to bolster Britain's financial position.

By September 1965 it was the turn of Gaullist France to make
economics the instrument of politics. For her to assist further in
shoring up the pound was also to help out the dollar—to reinforce, in
other words, that American leadership of the West with which Britain
was identified. The Bank of France decamped when the international
consortium renewed its support of sterling. In June 1966, however,
there had to be a fresh arrangement and France returned to the fold.
Undertakings by the United States and France were bilateral ones.

Protectionist elements are not the only ones that may be constrained by events to reassess American interests. There should also be much bipartisan soul-searching among liberals in the Executive and Legislative branches of the American government. For the new Europe has again illustrated how ventures that are progressive in theory can in practice be somewhat retrograde—how older links and traditional combines can, despite rigid liberal preconceptions, still be a safer means for accomplishing liberal ends.

What would be the larger consequences of a countervailing American initiative? An indispensable British ally might not only find in Washington an economic alternative to Brussels; overseas dislocations in the Commonwealth could also be arrested. Canada, Australia, and New Zealand might thereby reconcile defense commitments with the United States and attachments to Britain that are not merely economic. Even neutralist members of the Commonwealth might feel less isolated. As for the United States, if she has an interest in Britain as a European stabilizer, she must have a commensurate interest in overseas connections by which the strength of Britain in Europe may still be sustained. A sense of mutuality has banded them all together at decisive turning points in the twentieth century. That sense is what the United

---

The nine other members of the consortium now worked with and through the Bank of International Settlements. But the British people also had to subject themselves to stricter economic self-discipline. And that is what they are doing at last.

Meanwhile Washington had seen from the outset that short-term loans were not enough—that there would have to be a further modernization of British industry before an increase in British exports could more steadily redress the British balance of payments. Bonn and Paris opposed a massive long-term loan for this purpose. But if one sort of American initiative is blocked, another sort may have to be undertaken.

States, by a saving realignment under an American aegis, can revitalize and reaffirm.

But what about the Atlantic partnership that Presidents Kennedy and Johnson have advocated? This would not be the same as one in which Britain had been Europeanized. And yet its structure rather than its purpose is what would be modified. Then, too, a united Europe might be less self-willed when a countervailing American initiative is mounted. While the unification of Western Europe is an admirable objective, it must not override all others. Before the Common Market should come the common interest. The United States can do most to make that clear.

By some miracle, satisfactory arrangements may yet be reached in current economic negotiations. There would then be no need for a countervailing American initiative. But the political grounds that may make one necessary will be as valid as ever.

The Atlantic partnership that the United States has visualized could have immense scope by offering brokerage on every sector of policy. Such a partnership must, however, be one that is based on existing assets—one that fulfills the great desiderata of the age by preserving rather than destroying.

Divergences will yawn periodically between the United States and Britain. We study the past in vain if we do not expect that to occur. But the past also reveals what the entire free world owes to Anglo-American friendship—and history will not let off lightly those in Washington or in London who may be tempted to ignore its lessons.

Index